FOREWORD

The Hidden Places series is a collection of easy to use travel guides taking you, in this instance, on a relaxed but informative tour of Sussex. It is a county rich in heritage and endowed with attractive rolling hills and beautiful woodlands as well as a charming and picturesque coastline.

Our books contain a wealth of interesting information on the history, the countryside, the towns and villages and the more established places of interest in the county. But they also promote the more secluded and little known visitor attractions and places to stay, eat and drink many of which are easy to miss unless you know exactly where you are going.

We include hotels, inns, restaurants, public houses, teashops, various types of accommodation, historic houses, museums, gardens, garden centres, craft centres and many other attractions throughout Sussex, all of which are comprehensively indexed. Most places have an attractive line drawing and are cross-referenced to coloured maps found at the rear of the book. We do not award merit marks or rankings but concentrate on describing the more interesting, unusual or unique features of each place with the aim of making the reader's stay in the local area an enjoyable and stimulating experience.

Whether you are visiting the area for business or pleasure or in fact are living in the county we do hope that you enjoy reading and using this book. We are always interested in what readers think of places covered (or not covered) in our guides so please do not hesitate to use the reader reaction forms provided to give us your considered comments. We also welcome any general comments which will help us improve the guides themselves. Finally if you are planning to visit any other corner of the British Isles we would like to refer you to the list of other *Hidden Places* titles to be found at the rear of the book.

Travel Publishing

CONTENTS

1 Chichester and the West Sussex Coast

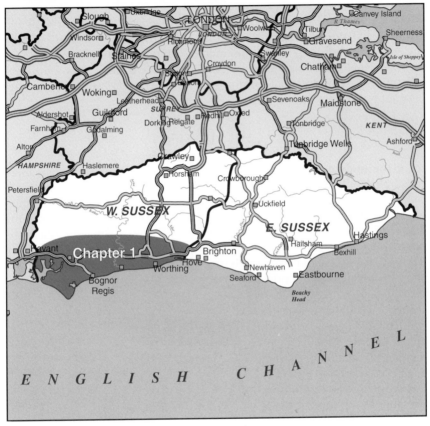

INTRODUCTION

This western, coastal region of West Sussex is centred around Chichester, the county town, Arundel, with its magnificent castle, and the resorts of Littlehampton, Bognor Regis and Worthing. An ecclesiastical centre for over 900 years, Chichester was founded by the Romans in the 1ˢᵀ century. Its fine, natural harbour, once a busy place for trade and also smugglers, is now a lively yachting centre with delightful old fishing villages found along its inlets. Nearby, at Fishbourne, the grateful Roman conquerors built a splendid palace for the Celtic King Cogidubnus who collaborated with the invaders. The largest estate north of the Alps, the Roman remains were only uncovered this century whilst a new water mains was being installed.

The inland town of Arundel is not only home to the marvellous castle situated beside the River Arun but also the area's second cathedral. Built by the Roman Catholic family living at the castle, Arundel Cathedral is famous for its Corpus Christi Festival.

Back to the coast and the stylish resorts of Littlehampton, Bognor Regis and Worthing. Overshadowed by their great rival to the east - Brighton - each of these once small fishing villages has much to offer in an unbrash and timeless manner. Finally, the small town of Selsey and Selsey Bill, the most southwesterly tip of West Sussex, is a charming place with as much history as there are pleasant walks along the coastline.

CHICHESTER

Set on the low lying plain between the south coast and the South Downs, Chichester, the county town of West Sussex, was founded by the Romans in the 1st century. The invading Roman legions used the town as a base camp, christening it *Noviomagus*, "the new city of the plain", and both the city walls and the four major thoroughfares - North, South, East and West Streets - follow the original Roman town plan. They cross at the point where a fine 16TH century **Butter Cross** now stands; an ornate structure built in 1500 by Bishop Edward Story to provide shelter for the many traders who came to sell their wares at the busy market.

The city walls, originally consisting of raised earthwork embankments built in an irregular 11-sided shape, were constructed around AD 200. Over the subsequent centuries alterations and improvements were made and, today, the remaining walls largely date from medieval times and large sections still form the boundary between the old and new city. After the Romans left, the Saxons came, in AD 500, and Chichester's modern name is derived from Cissa's ceaster after the Saxon King Cissa.

Chichester also has a long and colourful ecclesiastical his-

Chichester Cathedral

tory and, although St Wilfrid chose nearby Selsey as the site of the area's first cathedral, the conquering Normans, who moved all country bishoprics to towns, built a new cathedral on the present site in the late 11ᵀᴴ century. Resting on Roman foundations, the construction work began in 1091 and the finished building was finally consecrated in 1184. A fire, just three years later, all but destroyed the cathedral and a rebuilding programme was started by Richard of Chichester in the 13ᵀᴴ century. A venerated bishop who was canonised in 1262, Richard of Chichester was subsequently adopted as the city's patron saint.

Lying in the heart of the city, **Chichester Cathedral**, a centre for Christian worship for over 900 years, is unique on two counts. Firstly, it is the only medieval English cathedral that can be seen from the sea rather than being secluded by its own close and, secondly, it has a detached belfry. The existing tower was thought not to have been sturdy enough to take the cathedral bells and hence another separate building was needed. Indeed, in 1861, the cathedral spire blew down in a storm and demolished a large section of the nave. The present 277 foot spire was designed by Sir Gilbert Scott and, in keeping with the building's original style, it can also be seen for miles around from all directions.

Among the treasures within the cathedral is the Shrine of St Richard of Chichester along with some fine Norman arches, a set of 14ᵀᴴ century choir stalls and, surprisingly, some excellent modern works of art. There is an altar tapestry by John Piper, a stained glass window by Marc Chagall and a painting by Graham Sutherland of Christ appearing to Mary Magdalene. However, the most important treasures to be seen are the Norman sculptures: *The Raising of Lazarus* and *Christ Arriving in Bethany* which can be found on the south wall. The **Prebendal School**, the cathedral choir school, is the oldest school in Sussex and it stands alongside the main building.

From the Middle Ages until the 18ᵀᴴ century, Chichester was a major trading and exporting centre for the Sussex woollen trade and some handsome merchants' houses were built using these profits. The city's oldest building is **St Mary's Hospital**, dating from the 13ᵀᴴ century, which was established to house the deserving elderly of Chichester.

The almshouses that were built into the hospital walls are still inhabited and the chapel has some unique misericords. The city's **Guildhall**, built in the 1270s as the church of the Franciscans, is also well worth seeing. Later becoming Chichester's

Chichester Guildhall

town hall and law courts it was here, in 1804, that the poet William Blake was tried for treason and acquitted. Today, it is home to a display telling the story of the building and the surrounding Priory Park in which it stands.

There are also some fine Georgian buildings to be found here and, in the area known as The Pallants, lies **Pallant House**. A fine example of a red brick town house, it was built in 1713 by the local wine merchant Henry 'Lisbon' Peckham and the building is guarded by a wonderful pair of carved stone do-dos, which have given rise to its local nickname - the Dodo House. Another curious feature is the observation tower on the house from which Peckham would look out for his merchant ships returning laden with goods from the Iberian Peninsula. Today, the house is the **Pallant House Gallery**, one of the country's finest galleries outside London, and home to a modern art collection that includes works by Moore, Sutherland, Piper, Klée and Cèzanne.

One of the city's most distinctive modern buildings can be found at Oaklands Park, close by the city walls. The **Chichester Festival Theatre** was opened in 1962 and the splendid hexagonal building has since gained a reputation for staging the finest classical and contemporary drama, opera and ballet. A focal point of the annual Chichester Festival, along with the cathedral, for two weeks during July, the city is alive with a myriad of cultural events. For those with quieter interests, the **Mechanical Music and Doll Collection** represents a fas-cinating walk through the last 100 years of mechanical music. Playing the tunes of late 19TH century public houses through to genteel Victorian parlour songs, the beautifully restored instruments are put through their paces on a regular basis. Also to be seen with the collection are Edison phonographs, early horned gramophones, stereoscopic viewers and over 100 dolls spanning the years from 1830 to 1930.

Once a busy port, the city is now a haven for all boat lovers and yachtsmen, with a bustling harbour from which there are boat trips and, also, some fabu-lous yachts moored in the one of Europe's largest marinas. A particularly pleasant waterside walk can be taken from the city's impressive canal basin, along the **Chichester Canal** (all that now remains of a once longer waterway from Arundel to Portsmouth), to Chichester Harbour. The canal opened in 1822, taking ves-sels up to 150 tons, and the last commercial cargo travelled the route in 1928 but, following restoration work, it is a delightful walk that takes in some charm-ing views and there is a cruise boat on which to make the return journey.

Housed in an 18TH century corn store, **Chichester District Museum** explores local history through displays and hands-on activities. The journey starts back through time when visitors can find out about local geology and prehistory, including Boxgrove Man. Life in Roman, Saxon and medieval Chichester can also be discovered. The journey then continues upstairs where there are dis-plays on Chichester during the Civil War. Visitors can then see how the city changed during Georgian and Victorian times which also includes displays on

Chichester District Museum, 29 Little London, Chichester, West Sussex
PO19 1PB Tel: 01243 784683 Fax: 01243 776766
e-mail: chichmus@breathemail.net

the market. The story is brought up to date with displays on Chichester since 1900. The museum has a programme of changing exhibitions and there are a wide range of regularly held events for all ages including talks, walks and children's activities. There is also a small shop selling books, postcards and other souvenirs. A wonderful way to spend time while finding out about local life in the past, Chichester District Museum has no admission charge. Open Tuesday to Saturday, 10.00-17.30 (closed Sundays, Mondays and all Bank Holidays). There is also wheelchair access available to the ground floor only.

AROUND CHICHESTER

MID LAVANT
2 miles N of Chichester on the A286

MAP 1 REF C5

This attractive village, along with its neighbour East Lavant, is named after the small river which flows from Singleton into Chichester Harbour. There are spectacular views from here northwards over the South Downs and it is said that these were the inspiration for the words 'England's Green and Pleasant Land' which appear in William Blake's famous poem, *Jerusalem*.

GOODWOOD
MAP 1 REF C5
3 miles NE of Chichester off the A285

This is not a village but the spectacular country home of the Dukes of Richmond - **Goodwood House** - that was first acquired by the 1ˢᵀ Duke of Richmond (the natural son of Charles II and his beautiful French mistress, Louise de Keroualle) in 1697 so that he could ride with the local hunt. The rather ordinary brick residence was superseded by the present mansion that was built on a grand scale in the late 18ᵀᴴ century for the 3ᴿᴰ Duke by the architect James Wyatt. At the same time the splendid stables were added and the original, modest hunting lodge still remains in the grounds. Now refurbished by the Earl and Countess of March, several rooms in this impressive house, including the state apartments, are open to visitors and, among the items on display, are paintings by Canaletto and Stubbs, fine Sèvres procelain collected by the 3ᴿᴰ Duke whilst he was Ambassador to Paris, gruesome relics from the Napoleonic Wars and French and English furniture.

Viewers of the BBC television drama *Aristocrats* will recognise the house as it was used as the location for the series. Not only was the drama filmed here but the story was that of the independent minded and glamorous daughters of the 2ᴺᴰ Duke of Richmond. The girls grew up both at Goodwood House and at the Duke's London residence, Richmond House, and the whole family were enthusiastic leaders of early Georgian society. Goodwood House was the setting for Sarah's banishment from society and it was also here that Kildare wooed Emily. On display in the house is a painting by Stubbs which features Caroline's husband, Lord Holland, and the Meissen snuff box the couple gave to the duchess four years after their elopement.

The house is the focal point of the Goodwood Estate, some 12,000 acres of downland which also incorporate the world famous **Goodwood Racecourse**. A favourite venue with the rich, racing has taken place here for nearly 200 years and, in particular, there is the Glorious Goodwood meeting. First introduced by the 4ᵀᴴ Duke of Richmond in 1814, just 12 years after racing began here, this prestigious five day meeting is one of the major events in the calendar and has long been a much anticipated part of the summer season. Further, the estate contains a golf course, a motor racing circuit and a children's adventure play area.

HALNAKER
MAP 1 REF C5
3½ miles NE of Chichester on the A285

Pronounced Hannacker, this village was the seat of the influential and powerful De La Warr family. The present **Halnaker House**, designed by Edwin Lutyens in 1938, is a splendid modern country house. However, just to the north lies the original Halnaker House which was allowed to fall into decay around 1800 - just as the residents of nearby Goodwood House were commanding attention within London's society. Built in medieval times, the old house was originally the home of the De Haye family who were also the founders of Boxgrove Priory.

Above the village, on Halnaker Hill, stands an early 18ᵀᴴ century tower windmill, **Halnaker Windmill**, which remained in use until 1905 when it too was allowed to fall into ruin. In 1912, Hilaire Belloc mentioned the windmill in a poem where he compares the decay of agriculture in Britain with the neglected mill. The exterior, however, was restored in 1934 and the windmill was used as an observation tower during World War II.

BOXGROVE

MAP 1 REF C6

2 miles NE of Chichester off the A27

This attractive village is home to the remains of **Boxgrove Priory**, a cell of the Benedictine Lessay Abbey in France which was founded in around 1115. Initially a community of just three monks, over the centuries the priory expanded and grew into one of the most influential in Sussex. However, all that remains today are the Guest House, Chapter House and the Church which is now the parish Church of St Mary and St Blaise. Its sumptuous interior reflects the priory's former importance and, before the Dissolution of the Monasteries, the De La Warr Chantry Chapel was built like a 'church within a church' as the final resting place of family. Unfortunately, Henry VIII forced De La Warr to dispose of the priory and the family were eventually buried at Broadwater near Worthing. Though it is still empty, the extravagant marble chapel has survived.

A fascinating discovery was made, in 1993, by local archaeologists who unearthed prehistoric remains in a local sand and gravel pit. Amongst the finds was an early hominid thigh bone and, whilst there is still some debate over the precise age of the bone, the find has been named **Boxgrove Man**.

TANGMERE

MAP 1 REF C6

2 miles E of Chichester off the A27

The village is still very much associated with the nearby former Battle of Britain base, RAF Tangmere and, although the runways have now been turned back into farmland or housing estates, the efforts of those brave young men are remembered at the local pub, The Bader Arms (named after pilot Douglas Bader) and **Tangmere Military Aviation Museum**. The museum, based at the airfield, tells the story, through replica aircraft, photographs, pictures, models and memorabilia, of military flying from the earliest days during World War I to the present time. The Battle of Britain Hall tells its own story with aircraft remains, personal effects and true accounts from both British and German pilots of those desperate days in 1940. On display are also two historic aircraft, each of which beat the World Air Speed record on their day, actually at the Tangmere airfield. Finally, it was whilst at RAF Tangmere during World War II that EH Bates completed his novel *Fair Stood the Wind for France*.

SIDLESHAM

MAP 1 REF C6

4 miles S of Chichester on the B2145

A pleasant village that is home to an interesting information and interpretation centre for **Pagham Harbour Nature Reserve**. The harbour was formed when the sea breached reclaimed land in 1910 and it is now a well known breeding ground for many rare birds. The tidal mud flats not only attract an abundance of wildfowl but also many species of animals and marine life. Sidlesham Ferry is the starting point for guided walks around this important conservation area.

The picturesque **Crab and Lobster** public house occupies a quiet country lane in this lovely village. Dating back to the 1660s, this country pub is a welcoming haven of tranquillity with real character and oak beamed ceilings. The ambience is friendly and inviting, as owners Brian and Liz Cross have a knack for making every visitor feel special. Visitors too get a chance to meet Bentley and Porche, the couple's gentle Irish setters. Brian brings the benefit of his 37 years of experience to bear on maintaining just the right atmosphere of warmth and bonhomie. There are lovely, well tended gardens to the rear and two bars in which to enjoy a drink and a meal. For added curiosity value, the bar in the Ham Bar is part of an old fishing boat that was salvaged from the nearby mud flats some 50 years ago. As a free house, the choices of what to drink include four real ales. All the food is homemade and homeprepared;

The Crab and Lobster, Mill Lane, Sidlesham, near Chichester, West Sussex PO20 7NB Tel: 01243 641233

dishes range from steaks, fresh haddock and steak and kidney pie to Cantonese prawns and, of course, crab and lobster.

NORTON
MAP 1 REF C6
6 miles S of Chichester on the B2145

One of the original communities that made up Selsey (Sutton, the other, is now the present day town), Norton's first church was probably built on, or close to, the site of the cathedral that St Wilfrid erected when he became Bishop of the South Saxons in AD 681. Following the Norman Conquest, the country bishoprics were moved into the towns and Selsey's bishop transferred to Chichester. In the 1860s, the decision to move the medieval parish Church of St Peter from its isolated site to Selsey was taken. But, according to ecclesiastical law, a church chancel cannot be moved, so it remains here as **St Wilfrid's Chapel.**

SELSEY
MAP 1 REF C7
7 miles S of Chichester on the B2145

Once an important Saxon town, fishing has been the main stay of life here for many centuries. However, according to accounts by the Venerable Bede, St Wilfrid, whilst Bishop of the South Saxons, discovered that the Selsey fishermen were unsuccessful and such was their shortage of food that they were prepared to throw themselves off nearby cliffs. St Wilfrid taught them to fish and the town has thrived ever since and, until recently, only Selsey crabs were served on the QE2.

Now a more modest town yet still a popular resort, the main street still looks much as it did in the 18ᵀᴴ century. The **Sessions House**, where the Lord of Selsey Manor held court, was probably built in the early 17ᵀᴴ century though it still contains the exposed beams and wooden panelling of an earlier age. There are also several thatched cottages to be seen, including the 18ᵀᴴ century Century Cottage and the 16ᵀᴴ century farmhouse known as The Homestead. Perhaps, though, the most impressive building here is **Selsey Windmill**. Today's mill was built in 1820 as the previous late 17ᵀᴴ century timber construction had suffered greatly from weather damage. A tower mill built from local red bricks, though it ceased milling flour in 1910, the mill continued to grind pepper into the 1920s. Now rescued and restored it is a pleasant local landmark.

With so many of the townsfolk dependant upon the sea for their living, the Lifeboat Station was established here in 1860. The present building was erected 100 years later and there is also an interesting **Lifeboat Museum**.

For many years the town's **East Beach** was a well recognised scene for smuggling and, in the 18ᵀᴴ century, this was a full time occupation for many local inhabitants. In fact, whilst the French were in the throws of their revolution the villagers of Selsey were busy smuggling ashore over 12,000 gallons of spirits. Much later, during World War II, East Beach was used as a gathering point for sections of the famous Mulberry Harbour that was transported across the Channel as part of the D-Day landings. Just inland from the beach, now on a roundabout, is a small building called the **Listening Post**. During World War I it was used as a naval observation post, with personnel listening out for the sound of invading German airships, and as such it acted as an early warning system long before radar was established.

Just outside the town and situated around some fine old farm buildings is **Northcommon Farm Centre**. Offering an interesting day out for all the family, the centre has a wide selection of farm animals, including cows and calves, sheep and lambs, donkeys, goats and pigs as well as miniature ponies, horses and llamas. There are tractor and trailer rides to take visitors around this old farm.

Geographically, **Selsey Bill**, the extreme southwest of Sussex, is an island with the English Channel on two sides, Pagham Harbour to the northeast and a brook running from the harbour to Bracklesham Bay which cuts the land off from the remainder of the Manhood Peninsular. However, Ferry Banks, built in 1809, links the bill with the mainland. Over the centuries this part of the coastline has been gradually eroded and many of the area's historic remains have been lost beneath the encroaching tides.

The Rushmere is certainly a restaurant and bar with a difference. Originally a tea rooms, this typical early 1930s building has been completely refurbished by owner John Smyth, to provide customers with excellent personal service in a charming country home style setting. Surrounded by its own private well maintained gardens, with attractive borders and patios which make the perfect backdrop for a pre-dinner drink, The Rushmere is a place for relaxation where customers can indulge themselves in its intimate surroundings. As well as the garden, the large comfortable bar area is ideal for a drink before moving through

The Rushmere, Hillfield Road, Selsey, West Sussex PO20 9DB
Tel: 01243 605000 Fax: 01243 602602

to one of the two restaurant rooms. Both have been carefully decorated and furnished to provide elegant surroundings in which diners can enjoy the splendid menu that is put together from the very best seasonal produce by The Rushmere's own chef. Seafood is a house speciality and, to complement any meal, the wine waiter is on hand to suggest a suitable accompaniment. The combination of old world charm with a warm welcome, makes The Rushmere an exceptional place where a meal out is an experience to be savoured.

EARNLEY   Map 1 ref B6
6 miles SW of Chichester off the B2198

This charming small village is home to **Earnley Gardens**, a delightful place with 17 themed gardens, exotic birds and butterflies and also an unusual museum. **Rejectamenta**, the Museum of 20TH Century Memorabilia, displays thousands of everyday items which reflect the changes in lifestyle over the past 100 years. There is everything here from old washing powder packets and winklepickers to stylophones and space hoppers.

WEST WITTERING   Map 1 ref B6
7 miles SW of Chichester on the B2179

West Wittering and its larger neighbour, **East Wittering**, both lie close to the beautiful inlet that is Chichester's natural harbour. A charming seaside village, West Wittering overlooks the narrow entrance to the harbour and this former fishing village has developed into a much sought after residential area and select holiday resort. Here, too, lies **Cakeham Manor House**, with its distinctive early 16TH century brick tower that was once the summer palace of the bishops of Chichester. A splendid part medieval, part Tudor and part Georgian house, it was in the manor's studio that Sir Henry Royce, of Rolls Royce, designed many of his inventions.

Both villages have easy access to excellent sandy beaches and the headland that forms the eastern approach to Chichester Harbour, **East Head**, which is now a nature reserve. A sand and shingle spit which supports a variety of bird, plant and marine life, marram grass has been introduced to the sand dunes to help reduce the ravages of the sea and wind.

ITCHENOR   Map 1 ref B6
5 miles SW of Chichester off the B2179

Originally a Saxon settlement called Icenore, in the 13TH century the villagers of Itchenor built a church which they chose to dedicate to St Nicholas, the guardian of seafarers. As the village overlooks the sheltered waters of Chichester Harbour, shipbuilding was an obvious industry to become established here and, as early as the 1600s, there was a shipyard at Itchenor. The last ships built here were minesweepers during World War II but the village today is a busy sailing and yachting centre as well as being the customs clearance port for Chichester Harbour.

The aptly named **Ship Inn** is not only situated on the shores of Chichester Harbour but also just a few hundred yards from the jetty where local boat trips take visitors on a tour of the harbour. Though the pub today only dates from the 1930s, it was built on the site of the previous inn which has been serving the needs of the villagers and visiting seafarers since the early 18TH century. A warm and welcoming free house, owned and personally run by Roger Stearn and Silas Woolley, who both have local connections, this is the place to come to

**Ship Inn, Itchenor, near Chichester, West Sussex PO20 7AH
Tel & Fax: 01243 512284 e-mail: silas@packardbell.org**

for excellent food, drink and hospitality. The large bar area, from which a wide range of real ales, lagers and an interesting selection of wines are served, has a nautical theme and includes an interesting seat made from a section of a boat that was retrieved from Chichester Harbour and a weather station above the fireplace. Separately, but still with a nautical theme, the dining room is a comfortable and intimate area where visitors can enjoy a delicious meal from the mouthwatering menu of freshly prepared dishes. Not surprisingly, fresh local fish features heavily and is the house speciality. A popular pub with both locals and visitors, the Ship Inn provides a convivial and relaxing atmosphere for an evening out.

BIRDHAM
MAP 1 REF B6
4 miles SW of Chichester on the A286

The setting for Turner's famous painting of Chichester Harbour (which can be seen at Petworth House), this delightful place is as charming today as it was when the views captured the great artist's imagination. Here, too, can be found the **Sussex Falconry Centre**, which was originally set up as a breeding and rescue centre for indigenous birds of prey. In 1991, the centre started to exhibit the birds to the public and, as well as viewing and watching the birds fly, visitors can also take advantage of the centre's falconry and hawking courses.

FISHBOURNE
MAP 1 REF B6
2 miles W of Chichester on A286

This unremarkable village would not appear on anyone's list of places to visit in West Sussex if it was not for the splendid Roman remains that were only discovered in 1960 when a new water main was cut. **Fishbourne Roman Palace** was built around AD 75 for the Celtic King Cogidubnus, who collaborated with the Roman conquerors. As well as taking on the role of Viceroy, Cogidubnus was rewarded with this magnificent palace which contained underfloor heating, hot baths, a colonnade, an ornamental courtyard garden and lavish decorations. The largest residential building north of the Alps, among the superb remains are a garden and numerous mosaic floors, including the famous **Boy on a Dolphin** mosaic.

As well as walking through the excavated remains of the north wing, visitors can see the formal garden which has been replanted to the original Roman plan. When the palace was first constructed the sea came right up to its outer walls and the building remained in use until around AD 320 when a fire largely destroyed the site. The history of the palace, along with many of the artefacts rescued during the excavations, can be discovered in the **Museum**, where there is also an exhibition area on Roman gardening.

Dating back to the 17ᵀᴴ century, **The Bulls Head**, which was originally built as a farmhouse, is an attractive black and white inn that is also a listed building. Shortly after George Eastland, a sea captain from Chichester, was given a con-

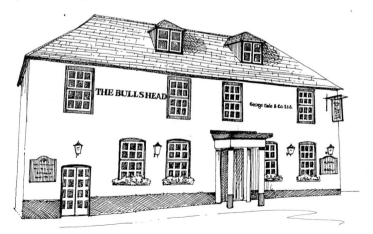

The Bulls Head, Fishbourne, Chichester, West Sussex PO19 3JP
Tel: 01243 839895 Fax: 01243 774647

gratulatory dinner here after surviving a bad storm he became the inn's first landlord and The Bulls Head has remained a licensed premises ever since then. Now managed by experienced partners, Julie Edwards and Roger Pocock, The Bulls Head has gained a reputation for the high standard of hospitality which both locals and visitors can expect. A warm and welcoming place, not only is there an excellent range of real ales on tap but this intimate country pub had a superb menu of reasonably priced dishes. All homecooked and prepared from fresh local ingredients the resident chef specialises in heart warming casseroles and interesting and unusual sauces. Those who are visiting the area will also be interested in the large family room that is available on a bed and breakfast basis that provides a level of accommodation that mirrors the delightful and characterful surroundings of the bar and dining room. However, it is for the monthly traditional jazz music, played the first Sunday in every month, for which The Bulls Head is particularly famous. Over the years the pub has played host to such famous names in jazz as Ronnie Scott and the inn remains the place for live jazz in the area.

BOSHAM

Map 1 ref C5

3½ miles W of Chichester off the A286

Pronounced Bozzum, this pleasant village is well known for both its history and its charm. Though it was the Irish monk Dicul who built a small religious house here, Bishop Wilfrid is credited with bringing Christianity to the area in AD 681 and Bosham is probably the first place in Sussex where he preached. Later, in the 10TH century, Danish raiders landed here and, amongst the items that they stole, was the church's tenor bell. As the Danes left and took to their boats, the remaining bells were rung to sound the all clear and to indicate to the villagers that they could leave the nearby woods and return to their homes. As the last peal of bells rang out, the tenor bell, in one of the Danish boats, is said to have joined in and, in doing so, capsized the boat. Both the bell and the sailors sank to the bottom of the creek and the place is

Bosham Quay and Church

now known as **Bell Hole**. Whether the story is true or not, Bosham certainly has its fair share of local legends as the village has strong associations with King Canute. It was here, on the shore, that the king, in the early 11ᵀᴴ century, is said to have ordered back the waves in an attempt to demonstrate the limits of his kingly powers. Canute's daughter is also buried in the once important Saxon parish church.

Later in the 11ᵀᴴ century, King Harold sailed from Bosham, in 1064, on his ill-fated trip to Normandy to appease his rival, William of Normandy, for the English throne. However, Harold's plans went awry when he was taken captive and made to swear to William to aid his claim to the crown - a promise which, famously, Harold did not keep. It was the breaking of the promise obtained under threat that caused William to set forth with his army a couple of years later. As a result, Harold's lands in Sussex were some of the first to be taken by the conquering army and Bosham church's spire can be seen alongside Harold's ship in the Bayeux Tapestry.

An important port in the Middle Ages and particularly, between the 1800s and the 20ᵀᴴ century, when it was alive with oyster smacks, today's Bosham is a place for keen yachtsmen as well as charming place to explore. The narrow streets that lead down to the harbour are filled with elegant 17ᵀᴴ and 18ᵀᴴ century flint and brick buildings amongst which is the **Bosham Walk Craft Centre**. This fascinating collection of little shops selling all manner of arts, crafts, fashions and antiques within a old courtyard setting, also holds craft demonstrations and exhibitions throughout the season.

WALDERTON

MAP 1 REF B5

6 miles NW of Chichester off the B2146

Just to the west of the village lies **Stansted House**, a splendid example of late 17ᵀᴴ century architecture. Dating back to the 11ᵀᴴ century when it was a hunting lodge, as well as having several interesting owners, Stansted has played host to a variety of distinguished guests, including royalty, over the centuries. The house, as seen today, was built on its present site in 1668 for Richard Lumley - probably by the architect William Talman. Heavily altered in the following two centuries, Stansted House was burnt to the ground in 1900 but, in 1903, the house was rebuilt to the exact plans of Richard Lumley's grand mansion.

Now open to visitors, on a limited basis, the house is home to the late Lord Bessborough's collection of paintings and furnishings, including some fine 18ᵀᴴ century tapestries. Meanwhile, the **Below Stairs Experience** transports visitors to the old kitchen, pantry, servants' hall, living quarters and wine cellars, whilst the surrounding grounds are renowned for their peace and tranquillity. Finally, the **Stansted Park Garden Centre**, found in the original walled garden and restored Victorian glasshouses of the estate, includes a palm house, camellia house, fernery and vine house.

Probably dating from the late 18ᵀᴴ century, **The Barley Mow** is an inn with an interesting history. Originally built as cottages with possibly a bakehouse, the buildings were sold, by auction, in January 1865 - the details of which are on display in the bar - and it became this charming local pub. Now a real country inn, owned and run by experienced licensees Colin and Lynne Ive, the interior of The Barley Mow has a comfortable and relaxed atmosphere where real open fires add extra warmth on cold winter's days. The walls are adorned

The Barley Mow, Walderton, near Chichester, West Sussex PO18 9ED
Tel: 01705 631321 Fax: 01705 631403

with hop bins, old photographs of the village and its inhabitants in days gone by, and a mass of equine memorabilia which can provide more than one interesting topic of conversation. From the bar are served a wide selection of real ales, as well as the usual beers, lagers and spirits and, with two chefs on the premises, the extensive menu of tasty homemade traditional pub fare and Sunday lunches have also made The Barley Mow a popular place for food. However, what makes the pub special is its Skittle Alley which, over the years, has been used as stabling, a bakery and as a home for the local Home Guard. Available to prebooked parties, this is an ideal way to spend an evening with friends and the special Skittle Supper menu ensures that no one goes hungry during the excitement.

EAST ASHLING   Map 1 ref B5
3 miles NW of Chichester on B2178

A couple of miles to the north of East Ashling lies **Kingley Vale National Nature Reserve**, home probably to the finest yew groves in Europe. A long lived species - 100 years is nothing in the life of a yew tree - the trees were protected until the mid 16ᵀᴴ century as they were used for making long bows, England's successful weapon against crossbows. Here at Kingley Vale, there are several 500 year old trees although most of the forest is made up of trees approaching their 100ᵀᴴ birthday. Towards the summit of **Bow Hill**, the trees give way to heather and open heathland and here a group of four Bronze Age burial mounds, known as the King's Graves or Devil's Humps, can be found.

Originally built as a forge in the 17ᵀᴴ century, **The Horse and Groom** is a charming old country pub surrounded by its own enclosed garden and with lovely views across the South Downs. Though an old building, the interior of the pub is much lighter and brighter than expected: not because the oak beams and low ceilings have gone, but because the old scrubbed pine furniture adds a breath of fresh air whilst being in keeping with the warm and intimate style of the bar. A free house, The Horse and Groom serves a regularly changing list of real ales, as well as the usual beers and lagers, and its cosy feel makes it a popular drinking place with both locals and visitors. However, it is the splendid cuisine,

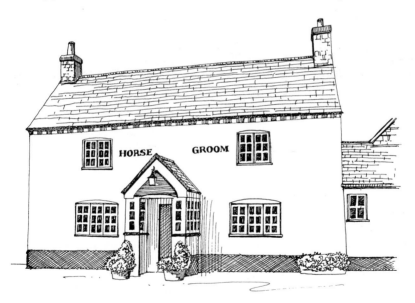

The Horse and Groom, East Ashling, Chichester, West Sussex PO18 9AX
Tel & Fax: 01243 575339

prepared by the French Chef and his team that has put owner Michael Martell's pub on the map of West Sussex. Naturally, there is a French influence to the dishes but there is certainly a magnificent choice, from tasty baguettes to gourmet meals, that is sure to please everyone. Add to this the inn's comfortable ensuite guest accommodation and it is easy to see why The Horse and Groom is gaining a well earned reputation for excellent hospitality.

ARUNDEL

A settlement since before the Romans invaded, this quiet and peaceful town, which lies beneath the battlements of one of the most impressive castles in the country, is a strategically important site where the major east-west route through Sussex crosses the River Arun. It was one of William the Conqueror's most favoured knights, Roger de Montgomery, who first built a castle here, on the high ground overlooking the river, in the late 11TH century. With a similar plan to that of Windsor castle, **Arundel Castle** consisted of a motte with a double bailey, a design which, despite several alterations and rebuildings, remains clearly visible today. The second largest castle in England, it has been the seat of the Dukes of Norfolk and the Earls of Arun for over 700 years.

Arundel Castle

Damaged in 1643 when, during the Civil War, Parliamentarian forces bombarded it with canons fired from the church tower, a programme of restoration took place during the late 18TH century to make it habitable once more. A second programme of rebuilding was undertaken 100 years later by the 15TH Duke of Norfolk, using profits from the family's ownership of the newly prosperous steel town of Sheffield. Unfortunately, all that remains today of the original construction are the 12TH century shell keep and parts of the 13TH century barbican and curtain wall.

However, despite the rebuilding work of the 18TH and 19TH century, the castle is still an atmospheric place to visit. The state apartments and main rooms contain some fine furniture dating from the 16TH century and there are some excellent tapestries and paintings by Reynolds, Van Dyck, Gainsborough, Holbein and Constable on show. Of the more personal items to be seen are the possessions of Mary, Queen of Scots and a selection of heraldic artefacts from the Duke of Norfolk's collection. The title, the Duke of Norfolk, was first conferred on Sir John Howard in 1483, by his friend Richard III, and, as well as carrying the hereditary office of Earl Marshal of England the Duke of Norfolk is also the premier duke of England.

Perhaps the most gruesome item to be seen at the castle can be found, not surprisingly, in the armoury. The **Morglay Sword**, which measures five feet nine inches long, is believed to have belonged to Bevis, a castle warden who was so tall that it was said he could walk from Southampton to Cowes without getting his head wet. In order to determine his final resting place, Bevis, so the story goes, threw his sword off the castle's battlements and, half a mile away, where the sword landed, is a mound that is still known as Bevis's Grave.

The period of stability that the castle brought to the town in the late medieval times turned Arundel into an important port and market town. In fact, the port of Arundel was mentioned in the Domesday Book and it continued to operate until the 20TH century when it finally closed in 1927 - the last Harbour Master was moved to Shoreham and the port transferred to Littlehampton.

It was also during this peaceful period that the 14TH century parish Church of St Nicholas was built, a unique church in that it is divided into separate Catholic and Anglican areas by a Sussex iron screen. Despite religious persecution, particularly during the 16TH century, the Fitzalan family and the successive Dukes of Norfolk remained staunch Catholics. So much so that the 15TH Duke, who was responsible for the 19TH century rebuilding of the castle, also commissioned the substantial Catholic Church of St Philip Heri which was designed by JA Hansom and Son, the inventors of the Hansom cab, in 1870. In 1965, this impressive building became the seat of the Catholic bishopric of Brighton and Arundel and was renamed the **Cathedral of Our Lady and St Philip Howard**. (Sir Philip was the 13TH Earl of Arundel who died in prison after being sentenced to death by Elizabeth I for his beliefs.) Each June, the cathedral hosts the two day Corpus Christi Festival during which the entire length of the aisle is laid out with a carpet of flowers.

Other historic sites in the town include the **Maison Dieu**, a medieval hospital outside one of the castle's lodges, that was founded by Richard Fitzalan in 1345. Dissolved by Henry VIII 200 years later, this semimonastic institution combined the roles of clinic, hotel and almshouse. For a greater insight into the history of the town and its various inhabitants down the ages, the **Arundel Museum and Heritage Centre** is well worth a visit. With imaginative use of models, old photographs and historic artefacts, the story of Arundel, from Roman times to the present day, is told.

Just to the north of the town, is the **Wildlife and Wetland Trust**, a wonderful place that plays host to a wide variety of ducks, geese, swans and other migratory birds from all over the world. There is a trail around the various lakes and ponds and an award winning visitor centre.

Found in the centre of the town, **Belinda's Restaurant** is an attractive and eyecatching old black and white building that is home to an excellent tea rooms and restaurant. The building itself has been found on an old town map of the mid 16TH century, when it was described as a barn, and remained so for many years before becoming a stable and slaughterhouse. During the 1920s, it was converted into a tea rooms though many of the original features, including a petrified oak doorpost, still remain to this day. Since then, further restoration

**Belinda's Restaurant, Tarrant Street, Arundel, West Sussex BN18 9DG
Tel: 01903 882977**

and renovation work has been carried out but visitors to Belinda's today can still see many of the original old timbers. Now owned and personally run by Christine and Vincent Farrell, this tea shop and restaurant is still a popular place with both locals and visitors to Arundel alike. Warm and cosy inside, with a friendly, relaxed atmosphere, customers can enjoy a whole range of homebaked cakes and breads that are made by Christine in the bakehouse at the rear of the shop. The menu also includes many other traditional favourites and the tasty menu of light meals and snacks is prepared from only the freshest local produce and ingredients and made to age old recipes. Belinda's is certainly the place to come to for a real taste of English homecooking.

Found beside the River Arun, just to the northeast of Arundel town centre, **The Black Rabbit** is a charming country inn in a splendid setting that has been providing excellent hospitality to river users and visitors alike for nearly 200 years. Originally built as an alehouse for those crewing boats on the Wey and Arun Canal (which closed in 1871), this attractive inn is now a popular place with both locals and tourists alike. As well as the long river frontage that is the ideal place to enjoy a drink on a lazy summer's day, the inn has a long and spacious bar that is light and airy in summer but added warmth is created in winter by the real log fires. Here, too, a traditional menu of pub food is served at both lunchtimes and in the evenings. For those who wish to make their visit to The Black Rabbit a more formal celebration there is a cosy restaurant where

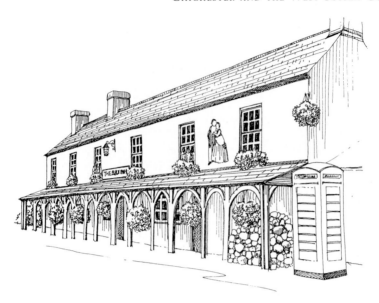

The Black Rabbit, Mill Road, Offham, Arundel, West Sussex BN18 9PB
Tel: 01903 882828 Fax: 01903 884278

diners can take fully advantage of the popular table d'hôte menu. Finally, it is believed that this is the only Black Rabbit inn in the country and the unusual name comes from the days when gamekeepers welcomed the sight of a black rabbit as it indicated that there were no poachers active in the area - black rabbits being easier to spot that the more usual light brown ones.

AROUND ARUNDEL

BURPHAM   MAP 1 REF D5
2 miles NE of Arundel off the A27

This charming and attractive downland village of flint and brick built thatched cottages overlooks the River Arun and provides excellent views of Arundel Castle. The peace and quiet found here seems far removed from the days when the Saxons built defensive earthworks in an attempt to keep the invading Danes at bay. Later, during the Middle Ages, one of the farms on nearby Wepham Down was a leper colony and the track leading down into the village is still known as Lepers' Way.

Following the brown information signs on the main A27 near Arundel railway station will bring the visitors to **The Burpham Country House Hotel**, the ideal place to get away from it all and take a Stress-Remedy Break. Parts of this

**The Burpham Country House Hotel, Burpham, near Arundel,
West Sussex BN18 9RJ Tel: 01903 882160 Fax: 01903 884627**

picturesque old house date back to 1710 and it stands amidst attractive and well maintained grounds. Reputed to have once been a hunting lodge for the Duke of Norfolk, today it is owned by George and Marianne Walker and, together, they have built up a fine reputation for offering first class accommodation, cuisine and service. Rapidly being acknowledged as one of West Sussex's top dining venues, Marianne, who is Swiss, supervises the dining room and the kitchen where she is ably assisted by her excellent chef, Stephen Piggott. All the dishes on the ever changing menu are prepared using only the best ingredients and can be accompanied by a fine wine from the extensive wine list. As well as the delightful dining room, guests can also dine in the new conservatory which overlooks the garden. The hotel also has its own cocktail lounge bar, where guests can relax on comfortable sofas in front of an open fire while enjoying a quiet pre-dinner drink. Most of the bedrooms enjoy lovely views of the South Downs; all have ensuite facilities and, as one would expect from a hotel of this calibre, are exquisitely furnished and superbly equipped. The Burpham Country House Hotel is an award winning hotel (Johansens "Most Excellent Service Award" for 1999 and silver award from the English Tourism Council) that comes highly recommended by all the leading guides.

LYMINSTER
1½ miles S of Arundel on the A284

MAP 1 REF D6

Lyminster is an ancient settlement of flint cottages and protective walls which appears, as *Lullyngminster*, in Alfred the Great's will of AD 901. From the village there is a marvellous view of Arundel Castle looking, this time, northwest across the water meadows of the lower River Arun. Local legend has it that the deep pool, known as the **Knuckler Hole**, which lies northwest of Lyminster church, was once inhabited by a savage sea dragon whose only food was fair maidens. This monster was said to have terrorised the local population to such an extent that the King of Wessex offered half his kingdom and his daughter's hand in marriage to the man who killed the beast. The dragon was finally slain after a terrible fight though there is some confusion regarding the identity of the brave dragon slayer. This was either a gallant ,young farm boy known as Jim Pulk or a handsome knight. Both stories, however, agree that the early Norman coffin slab in the north transept of the church is where the conquering hero was finally laid to rest and it is still known as the **Slayer's Stone**.

LITTLEHAMPTON
MAP 1 REF D6
3 miles S of Arundel on the A284

This is a charming maritime town, at the mouth of the River Arun, that is also an ancient site - signs of Roman occupation have been discovered here and the local manor is mentioned in the Domesday Book. Following the Norman invasion, Littlehampton became an important Channel port (declining considerably in the 1500s), exporting timber from the Sussex Weald and importing stone from Caen, France. It was here, too, that Queen Matilda arrived from France, in 1139, to stake her unsuccessful claim to the English throne from Stephen.

Now a quiet and pleasant coastal town and a popular holiday resort, though not as fashionable as many of its larger neighbours, Littlehampton does have all the ingredients for a traditional seaside break. There is a large amusement complex, a boating marina, a promenade and a harbour, where **Littlehampton Fort** can also be found. Built in 1764 in the shape of a crescent it is now hidden by vegetation. However, the town's most charming feature is, undoubtedly, the large green which lies between the seafront and the first row of houses.

Found in the old manor house in Church Street, **Littlehampton Museum** tells the history of the town, including its maritime past, through a series of informative displays. Also worthy of a visit is the **Body Shop Tour**, which takes place each Friday throughout the summer. The Body Shop Headquarters lie just outside the town, which is the birthplace of both the company and its founder Anita Roddick, and the tour shows visitors just how some of the company's environmentally and animal friendly products are made.

FORD
MAP 1 REF D6
2½ miles S of Arundel off the A259

Situated on an ancient ford crossing of the River Arun - as its name suggests - this village is dwarfed by a prison that is built on the site of an old RAF station which featured in the Battle of Britain. However, this does little to spoil the splendid and isolated setting of the old **Saxon parish church** that stands alone by the river.

Found next door to Ford's railway station, **The Shaky Doo** is a large mid Victorian pub that was, until World War II, called The Arundel Arms. During the war, the adjacent station was a target for enemy bombers but fortunately, one night, a bomb missed the station but landed in the pub's garden - where there is now a courtyard. Ever since, the pub has been known as The Shaky Doo as this was the name for a missed bomb. Now, in more peaceful times, the pub is owned and personally run by Marie Beattie with the help of her parents Joe and Mary Beattie. The family are from the west of Ireland and, though they

The Shaky Doo, Ford Road, Ford, Arundel, West Sussex BN18 0BH
Tel: 01903 882244

have much combined experience in the trade both here and at home, they have lost none of their Irish warmth and charm. The main attraction here, as well as the comfortable and interesting surroundings, can be found behind the bar as The Shaky Doo serves Dublin brewed Guinness for which people will travel miles. There is, of course, a whole range of other real ales, beers and lagers available at the bar. Food too is important and again there is an Irish influence. The breakfast bar, serving traditional Irish and English breakfast fare is open from 07.00 throughout the day whilst the other lunch and evening menus feature a mouthwatering range of delicious dishes prepared using Joe's homegrown organic vegetables. Fish is very much a house speciality and much is caught locally. As well as the delightful dining room, the excellent company, the delicious food and superb beers, The Shaky Doo regularly hosts live Irish music evenings - another reason to seek out this wonderful place. Finally, The Shaky Doo offers bed and breakfast accommodation in well appointed ensuite bedrooms so visitors can enjoy the delights of this place for longer.

FELPHAM

MAP 1 REF C6

5 miles SW of Arundel off the A259

This is the village to which the poet and artist, William Blake, moved to, along with his wife and sister, in 1800 in order to undertake some engraving work for William Hayley, a gentleman of the period. The cottage where the Blakes lived can still be seen down Blake's Road and it was also whilst here that he wrote 'Away to sweet Felpham for Heaven is there' which recalls the view of the sea from his window. He left the village a few years later after being tried and acquitted of sedition in Chichester.

BOGNOR REGIS

MAP 1 REF C6

6 miles SW of Arundel on the A259

Towards the end of the 18TH century Sir Richard Hotham, a wealthy London milliner, sought to transform Bognor from a quiet fishing village into a fashionable resort to rival Brighton. He set about constructing some imposing residences, including The Dome in Upper Bognor Road, and even planned to have the town renamed Hothampton. Unfortunately, the fashionable set of the day stayed away and Hotham's dream was never realised - at least not in his lifetime. However, in 1929, George V came to the resort to convalesce following a serious illness and, on the strength of his stay, the town was granted the title Regis (meaning of the King). Today, the town is a pleasant coastal resort with some elegant Georgian features, traditional public gardens, a promenade and safe, sandy beaches. The large central **Hotham Park** is another feature of this charming town where visitors can enjoy concerts given at the bandstand, clock golf, tennis and strolling around the naturally planted areas. The **Bognor Regis Museum**, housed in a lodge of Hotham Park, plays tribute to Sir Richard Hotham as well as telling the story of the famous bathing machine lady, Mary Wheatland, and the important stay of George V. Mary Wheatland was a well known Bognor Regis character: born in 1835 in the nearby village of Aldinbourne she would hire out bathing machines as well as teach children to swim and she also saved many souls from drowning for which she received medals and recognition from the Royal Humane Society. The sea air and exercise must have done the eccentric lady a great deal of good as she lived to be 89 years old.

Perhaps, more than anything else, the resort is known for its "Birdmen" and the annual international **Birdman Rally** held in August. The competitors, in a variety of classes, take it in turns to hurl themselves off the pier in an attempt to make the longest unpowered flight and so win the coveted competition.

YAPTON

MAP 1 REF D6

3½ miles SW of Arundel on the B2233

Set amid the wheatfields of the coastal plain, this village has a charming 12TH century church, the tower of which leans at an alarming angle.

Originally built as a cottage between 1720 and 1750, **The Lamb Inn** first became an ale house in the mid 19th century. Very much a traditional country inn, this attractive pub can be found on the south side of the village where there is not only plenty of parking space but also a large garden, with children's play area, and a separate enclosure for the pub's goats, ducks, geese and chickens. The interior of the lovely old inn is as delightful as the outside views would suggest - the wooden floors, inglenook fireplace and displays of horse brasses all

The Lamb Inn, Bilsham Road, Yapton, near Arundel, West Sussex BN18 0JN Tel: 01243 551232

add to the atmosphere and character. The Lamb Inn has been run by Jo and John since 1993 and they have certainly made their mark in the village. Very much the typical village pub, not only can customers enjoy an excellent pint of real ale here but there is always good conversation and plenty of traditional pub games to play. The food here too is of the same high standard and their Sunday lunches are considered by many to be the best roasts in the area - booking is therefore essential. Otherwise, during the rest of the week, the mouthwatering menu of traditional pub fare is well worth trying as all the dishes are freshly prepared from the very best local ingredients.

WALBERTON
Map 1 ref C6

3 miles W of Arundel off the B2132

Found down a narrow country lane, this pleasant village has obviously been settled for centuries as the parish church is built on Saxon foundations and it still contains an ancient Saxon tub shaped font.

Found tucked away in this quiet village off the beaten track is **The Holly Tree**, a delightful inn that can certainly call itself a hidden place. Very much a pub for the locals, few visitors to the area manage to find their way here. Thought to be an original 17TH century ale house, The Holly Tree does have plenty of olde worlde charm and character. There are roaring log fires in winter and several cosy rooms within that provide customers with intimate surroundings to enjoy

**The Holly Tree, The Street, Walberton, near Arundel,
West Sussex BN18 0PH Tel: 01243 554023**

a quiet drink, a chat and some food. As well as serving a splendid selection of everchanging real ales, all the usual range of beers, lagers and other drinks are available from the bar. Whilst host John Whitney is busy seeing to customers liquid refreshment, June, his partner, is busy in the kitchen. The menu here is all homecooked, by June, and her pies, particularly the salmon and prawn, are very popular, as too are the roast Sunday lunches. Using only the freshest, local ingredients, June selects her own fish from Littlehampton, a meal here is certainly a treat. However, this is not all that John and June offer their customers and, as this is a great meeting place for the local inhabitants, there are numerous events going on throughout the year including quiz nights and a whole host of team games.

FONTWELL

MAP 1 REF C6

3½ miles W of Arundel off the A27

The village is well known to followers of horse racing as it is home to the pleasantly situated **Fontwell Park National Hunt Racecourse**. First opened in 1921, the unusual 'figure of eight' track holds 15 meetings between August and May and remains a firm favourite with jumping enthusiasts. Fontwell is also home of **Denman's Garden**, a beautifully sheltered, semi-wild, 20TH century garden where the emphasis in planting has been put on colour, shape and texture which can be seen all year round.

SLINDON   MAP 1 REF C5

3 miles NW of Arundel off the A29

With a dramatic setting on the side of a slope of the South Downs, this pretty village has been occupied as an excellent observation point right from Neolithic times and many fine examples of early flint tools have been found in the area. The name itself is derived from the Saxon word for sloping hill. With splendid views over the coastal plain to the English Channel and numerous superb cottages, a visit here is well worth while.

The picturesque village of Slindon stands on a shelf of the South Downs and it was the estate village for Slindon House. Today, the **Slindon Estate** is owned by the National Trust and most of the village, the woodlands and Slindon House (now let to Slindon College) come under its care. The largest Trust owned estate in Sussex, there is plenty to see here as well as excellent opportunities for walking and birdwatching. Slindon House was originally founded as a residence for the Archbishops of Canterbury. (Archbishop Stephen Langton, a negotiator and signatory of the Magna Carta, spent the last weeks of his life here in 1228.) Rebuilt in the 1560s and extensively remodelled during the 1920s, the house is now a private boys' school. The estate's wonderful post office is an amalgamation of two 400 year old cottages and it is the village's only remaining thatched building. The focal point of the village is the crossroads where a tree stands in a small open area close to the village church. Dating from the 12TH century, this charming flint built church contains an unusual reclining effigy of a Tudor knight, Sir Anthony St Leger, the only wooden carving of its kind in Sussex. Finally, just to the north lies the cricket field where Sir Richard Newland is said to have refined the modern game over 200 years ago.

From the village there is a splendid walk around the estate that takes in the ancient deer park of Slindon House as well as other remains such as the summerhouse. The magnificent beech trees found in the woodland were once highly prized and their seeds were sold worldwide. Unfortunately, the severe storm of October 1987 flattened many of these splendid trees, some of which had stood for 250 years. Though most were cleared, some of the fallen trees were left and the dead wood has provided new habitats for a whole range of insects and fungi. Birds and other wild life also abound in the woodlands and, in May, the woodland floor is a carpet of bluebells.

Also at the Slindon Estate is **Gumber Bothy Camping Barn**, a stone tent that has been fully restored by the National Trust which now provides simple overnight accommodation just off the South Downs Way. Originally an out-

Gumber Bothy Camping Barn, Estate Office, Slindon, near Arundel, West Sussex BN18 0RN Tel: 01243 814730

building of Gumber Farm, a secluded working farm in the folds of the South Downs, the bothy is available to anyone over the age of five who enjoys the outdoor life. Sleeping up to 27 in three dormitory style rooms, the other facilities include showers, a drying room, a well equipped kitchen and a common room. For those who prefer there is a field for campers and, though no dogs are allowed, sociable horses can be accommodated overnight in a shared paddock.

EARTHAM   Map 1 ref C5
5 miles NW of Arundel off the A285

The village was the home of the 19TH century Member of Parliament, William Huskisson, the gentleman who was famously knocked down by Stevenson's *Rocket* during its inaugural run in 1830. Thus, Huskisson was able to claim the dubious honour of being the world's first recorded victim of a railway accident.

WORTHING

Despite having been inhabited since the Stone Age, Worthing remained a small and isolated fishing community until the end of the 18TH century when the popularity of sea bathing among the rich and fashionable set led to a period of rapid development. The climax to this period of development occurred in 1798, when George III sent his 16 year old daughter, Princess Amelia, to Worthing to recuperate from an ill-fated affair with one of his royal equerries. By 1830, however, Worthing's Golden Age was at an end but fortunately many of the Georgian town houses, villas and streets can still be seen today, just as they were nearly 200 years ago. Further development work was hampered by the cholera and typhoid outbreaks of the 1850s and 1890s although, between the two World Wars, some more modest expansion was undertaken.

Throughout much of the 19TH century, Worthing remained a popular resort with both royalty and the famous: it was here, in the summer of 1894, that Oscar Wilde wrote *The Importance of Being Ernest* and immortalised its name in that of the central character, Jack Worthing. Worthing's **Pier**, one of the country's oldest, was built in the 1860s as a pier was a must for any successful Victorian seaside resort. An elegant construction with a 1930s pavilion at the end, it has, during its lifetime, been blown down, burnt down and blown up! Of the more recent buildings to be found here, the **English Martyrs Catholic Church**, just west of the town centre, is a recommended stopping point as, painted on the ceiling, is a replica of Michelangelo's Sistine Chapel fresco that was completed by a local artist in 1993.

Today, Worthing is a bustling seaside town, with all the usual amenities necessary for a true English holiday as well as excellent shopping, dining and entertainment facilities. It also plays host to the **National Bowls Championships** that take place in Beach House Park.

Situated on the A259 Brighton Road and occupying a prominent position overlooking Steyne Gardens and the seafront, yet conveniently near to the main shopping centre, **Worthing Art and Craft Centre** is also within easy reach of town car parks and is gaining a reputation for high quality works of art and

Worthing Art and Craft Centre, 6 The Broadway, Brighton Road, Worthing, West Sussex BN11 3EG Tel: 01903 824999 e-mail: wacc@globalnet.co.uk

craft. Its attractive, well lit showroom displays original, handmade items from over 40 talented craftspeople and its art gallery offers customers the opportunity to browse in comfort with a cup of coffee or tea and homemade cakes in its elegant coffee shop.

The centre welcomes visitors seeking the illusive individuality that modern day shopping outlets cannot provide: ceramics, pottery, sculpture, jewellery, glassware, woodware, dried flowercraft, cards and much more await the discerning visitor. Furthermore, if the Worthing Art and Craft Centre does not have what the customer is looking for, they can arrange for it to be made especially for the customer. The Worthing Art and Craft Centre promises to find that special something for that special someone!

For a real insight into the history of this town a visit to the **Worthing Museum and Art Gallery** is essential. Through a series of fascinating displays, tales of smuggling, the town riots of the 19th century, top secret activities during World War II and the early life of this fishing village are told. The museum is also home to a nationally important costume and toy collection and, in the surrounding grounds, there is a sculpture garden.

As Worthing expanded it also swallowed up a number of ancient nearby settlements including Broadwater with its fine cottages and Norman church and West Tarring where the remains of a 13th century palace belonging to the Archbishops of Canterbury now double as the village hall and primary school annexe.

AROUND WORTHING

HIGH SALVINGTON
MAP 1 REF E6

1½ miles N of Worthing on the A24

This village, now almost entirely engulfed by Worthing, is home to the last survivor of several windmills that once stood in the area. **High Salvington Windmill**, a black post mill, was built between 1700 and 1720 and its design is one that had been used since the Middle Ages - a heavy cross shaped base with a strong central upright (or post) around which the sails and timber superstructure could pivot. The mill stopped working in 1897 but, following extensive restoration in the 1970s, it has now been restored to full working order and visitors can not only enjoy seeing this magnificent building as it was but also take afternoon tea and marvel at the glorious views.

FINDON
MAP 1 REF E5

3 miles N of Worthing off the A24

An attractive village, even though the heavily restored 13th century village church now lies on the opposite side of the main road, Findon's main square is surrounded by some elegant 18th century houses. Situated within the South Downs Area of Outstanding Natural Beauty, Findon is famous for being the venue of one of the two great Sussex sheep fairs - the other is at Lewes. Dating back to the days of the 13th century when the first markets were held here on Nepcote

Green, the annual **sheep fair** takes place each September and, as well as giving the village a festival atmosphere, over 20,000 sheep change hands here.

From Findon there is also easy access to **Cissbury Ring**, the largest Iron Age hillfort on the South Downs. Overshadowed only by Dorset's Maiden Castle, this impressive hilltop site covers an area of 65 acres and is surrounded by a double rampart almost a mile in circumference. Archaeologists have estimated that over 50,000 tons of chalk, soil and boulders would have had to be moved in the fort's construction which would indicate that this was once a sizeable community in the 3RD century BC. However, the site is much older than this as Neolithic flint mines have also been discovered here that date back 6000 years which also makes Cissbury one of the oldest industrial sites in the country. Today, the site is owned by the National Trust and is open to the public.

Though the origins of **The Gun Inn** are obscure studies made of the fabric of the building in the 1990s show that the original building dates from the mid 15TH century. However, the more recent history of this impressive old pub is much clearer and, from the first mention of The Muskett Gunn Inn in 1619 to

**The Gun Inn, High Street, Findon, near Worthing,
West Sussex BN14 0TA Tel: 01903 873206**

the present day, the story has been complied into an absorbing leaflet. Today's owner, Nick Hajibeorgiou, has been here a relatively short time - since 1998 - but he is also making his mark at The Gun Inn as well as in the village. A wonderful old place, with a charming Georgian frontage, the interior is typical of an English country inn. There are heavily beamed low ceilings, plenty of comfortable seats and a mass of pictures taken of the village which span the 20TH

century. A free house offering an excellent selection of real ales, including local brews, The Gun Inn also offers its customers a delicious menu of homecooked bar snacks and meals. All freshly prepared from local ingredients there are homemade soups and pies as well as a fine choice of meat, fish and vegetarian dishes to tempt customers. Not surprisingly, this is a popular inn and a warm welcome is extended to everyone - locals and visitors alike.

COOMBES
4 miles NE of Worthing off the A27
MAP 1 REF E5

This tiny settlement of just a few houses and a farm is worthy of a visit if just to see the **village church**, which stands in the farmyard. An unassuming Norman church it contains some exceptional 12TH century murals that were only uncovered in 1949 and are believed to have been painted by monks from St Pancras Priory, Lewes. Just to the north of the hamlet lies **Annington Hill** from where there are glorious views over the Adur valley and also there is access to a section of the South Downs Way footpath.

SHOREHAM-BY-SEA
4½ miles E of Worthing on the A259
MAP 2 REF E6

There has been a harbour here, on the River Adur estuary, since Roman times and, though evidence of both Roman and Saxon occupations have been found, it was not until the Norman period that the town developed into an important port. At that time the River Adur was navigable as far as Bramber and the main port was situated a mile or so upstream, where the Norman church of St Nicholas still stands.

However, towards the end of the 11TH century, the river estuary began to silt up and the old port and toll bridge were abandoned in favour of New Shoreham, which was built at the river mouth. Again, the Normans built a church close to the harbour and both churches remain key features of the town. The old town lapsed into the life of a quiet village whilst, during the 12TH and 13TH centuries, New Shoreham was one of the most important Channel ports. It was here, in 1199, that King John landed with an army to succeed to the throne of England following the death of Richard the Lionheart and, in 1346, Shoreham was asked to raise 26 ships, more than both Dover and Bristol, to fight the French. Perhaps, though, the town's most historic moment came in 1651 when Charles II fled from here to France, following defeat at the Battle of Worcester, on board the ship of Captain Nicholas Tettersell.

The new port flourished until the 16TH century when, once again, silting, in the form of a shingle spit which diverted the river's course, had disastrous economic consequences. The next 200 years or so saw a period of decline in Shoreham which was only relieved by the rise in popularity of nearby Brighton and the excavation of a new river course in 1818. To reflect its new importance,

Shoreham Fort was constructed at the eastern end of the beach as part of Palmerston's coastal defence system. A half-moon shape, the fort was capable of accommodating six guns which could each fire 80 pounds of shot. The fort has been restored and is now open to visitors who will also have a superb view of the still busy harbour.

The history of Shoreham-by-Sea and, in particular, its maritime past, are explored at **Marlipins Museum**. The museum is, itself, interesting, as it is housed in one of the oldest surviving non religious buildings in the country. A Norman customs warehouse, the building was given, in the 14ᵀᴴ century, an unusual knapped flint and Caen stone chequerwork façade and it has a single 42 foot beam supporting the first floor.

Though the town's past is, undoubtedly, built upon its port **Shoreham Airport**, opened in 1934, is the country's oldest commercial airport. Still a major base for recreational flying, the lovely art deco terminal acts as a departure and arrivals hall for many business passengers travelling to and from the Channel Islands and Western Europe. Also here, housed in a World War II blister hangar, is the **Museum of D-Day Aviation**. With a unique collection of early aircraft and artefacts, uniforms and medals from the desperate days of 1940, this is an interesting and unusual place to visit. Tours of the airport can also be booked.

NORTH LANCING   Map 1 ref E6
3 miles E of Worthing off the A27

This attractive downland village, with its curved streets, has one of the most ancient Saxon names in Sussex. It is derived from Wlencing, one of the sons of Aella, who led the first Saxon invasion to the area in AD 477. Apart from the old flint cottages on the High Street, the old 13ᵀᴴ century church adds to the timeless atmosphere of the village. However, North Lancing is dominated by a much more recent addition to its skyline - **Lancing College**. Set high up on a beautiful site overlooking the River Adur, the college was founded in 1848 by Nathaniel Woodward, whose aim was to establish a group of classless schools. By the time of his death in 1891, there were 15 schools in the

Lancing Chapel

Woodward Federation and, today, Lancing College is an independent secondary school. Of the college buildings, the splendid 19ᵀᴴ century Gothic style

Chapel is the most striking and it is considered to be one of the finest examples of its kind.

SOMPTING MAP 1 REF E6
2 miles E of Worthing off the A27

This village, the name of which means marshy ground, has, as its pride and joy, a church that is unique in Britain. Built on foundations which can be traced back to AD 960, the **Church of St Mary** has a distinctive spire that consists of four diamond shaped faces which taper to a point. Known as a Rhenish helm, the design was popular in German Rhineland but is not found elsewhere in this country. In 1154, the church was given to the Knights Templar who completely rebuilt it except for the spire which they left untouched. Just over 150 years later the building came into the hands of their rivals, the Knights Hospitallers, who were responsible for the present design of the church as they returned it to its original Saxon style.

GORING-BY-SEA MAP 1 REF E6
1½ miles W of Worthing on the A259

Until the arrival of the railway in the mid 19TH century, this was a small fishing village. However, the Victorians love of a day by the seaside saw the rapid growth of Goring and today it is a genteel place with a pleasant suburban air.

To the northwest stands the cone-shaped **Highdown Hill**, which, although only 266 feet high, stands out above the surrounding coastal plain. Its prominent nature has led it to be a much sought after vantage point and, over the centuries, it has been an Iron Age hillfort, a Roman bath house and a Saxon graveyard. The exceptional white painted country house, on the northern side of the hill, is **Castle Goring** and it was built in this elaborate Italian style for the grandfather of the poet Percy Bysshe Shelley.

Close by is **Highdown Gardens**, the creation of Sir Frederick and Lady Stern, who spent over 50 years turning what was originally a chalk pit into this splendid garden. One of the least known gardens in the area, Highdown has a unique collection of rare plants and trees which the couple brought back from their expeditions to the Himalayas and China in the mid 20TH century. The garden was left to the local borough council on the death of Sir Frederick in 1967 and it has been declared a national collection.

2 The West Sussex Downs

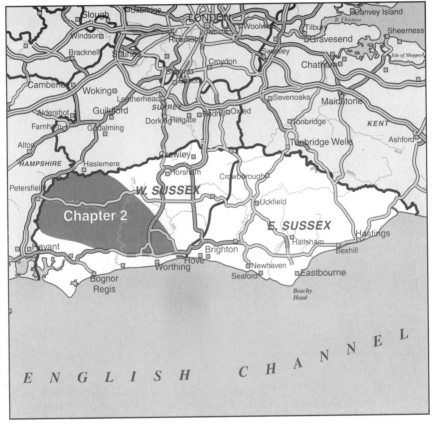

INTRODUCTION

The southern boundary to this part of West Sussex is the South Downs, a magnificent range of chalk hills that extend for over 100 miles and where the rolling countryside is grazed by sheep and cattle. The South Downs Way, a long distance bridleway follows the crest of the hills from Winchester to Beachy Head at Eastbourne and, whether taken as a whole or enjoyed in sections, it provides splendid views of this Area of Outstanding Natural Beauty as well as a wealth of delightful rural hamlets and villages to discover.

To the north of the Downs lies Midhurst, the home of the area's most famous ruin - Cowdray Park. Though the once splendid Tudor mansion has been reduced to a burnt out shell following a fire in the late 18ᵀᴴ century, the ruins provide a haunting backdrop to the parkland's famous polo matches. Fortunately, not all the grand country houses in this western part of the county have succumbed to flame and, in particular, there is Uppark, where HG Wells spent many hours in the great library as a boy and Petworth House, an elegant late 17ᵀᴴ century building that is very reminiscent of a French château.

Other great names from the world of the arts have also found this region inspirational and, whilst HG Wells is linked with Midhurst, the novelist Anthony Trollope spend his last years at South Harting, the poet Tennyson lived under the wooded slopes of Black Down and the composer Edward Elgar visited Fittleworth several times and wrote his famous cello concerto whilst staying there in 1917.

MIDHURST

Though this quiet and prosperous market town has its origins in the early Middle Ages, its name is Saxon and suggests that once it was surrounded by forest. It was the Norman lord, Savaric Fitzcane, who first built a fortified house here, on the summit of St Ann's Hill, and, though only a few stones remain today, the views from this natural vantage point over the River Rother are worth the walk.

The town of Midhurst grew up at the castle gates and by 1300, when the de Bohuns (the then lords of the manor) moved from their hilltop position the town was well established. Choosing a new site by the river in a coudrier, or hazel grove, gave the family the name for their new estate - **Cowdray**. In the 1490s, the estate passed, by marriage, to Sir David Owen, the natural son of Owen Glendower, and from then on until his death in 1535, Sir David built the splendid Tudor courtyard mansion. However, due to rising debts he was forced to sell the house to Sir William Fitzwilliam, a leading figure in the court of Henry VIII and the 1ˢᵀ Earl of Southampton. The finishing touches were added by him and his family and, when complete, the magnificent house was a great rival to

Cowdray Ruins, Midhurst

Hampton Court. Indeed, the house played host to many notable visitors including both Henry VIII and Elizabeth I who were frequently entertained here. Even though the house is in ruins following a devastating fire in 1793, it is still a splendid monument to courtly Tudor architecture. Today, visitors can view the roofless remains of the east side of the quadrangle court, along with parts of the west side where the turreted three storey gatehouse still remains largely intact. However, most visitors come to **Cowdray Park** to watch the polo matches that take place every weekend and sometimes during the week from April until July.

Back in the town, on the opposite side of the River Rother from Cowdray Park, there are also some impressive buildings including the 16th century timber framed **Market Hall** which is now the home of the famous **Midhurst Grammar School** that was founded in 1672. **The Spread Eagle Inn**, an old coaching inn, is, however, older and dates from the 1400s. Though the centre of the town has migrated away from its old heart around the market square and the church, the custom of ringing the curfew each night at 20.00 from the heavily restored church continues and is said to be in memory of a legendary commercial traveller. Whilst endeavouring to reach Midhurst, the traveller got lost in the local woods at dusk and, on hearing the sound of the church bells, was able to find his way safely to the town.

For most people visiting Midhurst, it is through the books of HG Wells that they feel that they already know the town. Wells' maternal grandmother came from Midhurst and his mother worked at nearby Uppark where, as a young boy, Wells spent many hours in the library. At the age of 15, Herbert George was apprenticed to a chemist in the town and also enrolled at the Grammar School for evening classes. Though he left Midhurst for some years, Wells later returned to the Grammar School as a teacher and, as well as providing the inspiration for his most famous book *The Invisible Man*, Midhurst has been the setting for many of his short stories including *The Man Who Could Work Miracles*. The great novelist and science fiction writer obviously had fond recollections of his time in the town for he wrote in his autobiography: 'Midhurst has always been a happy place for me. I suppose it rained there at times, but all my memories of Midhurst are in sunshine.'

AROUND MIDHURST

EASEBOURNE
1 mile N of Midhurst on the A272

MAP 1 REF C4

This delightful estate village, which has some superb half timbered houses, was the home of an Augustinian convent of the Blessed Virgin Mary. Founded in the 13th century, the convent prospered until 1478, when the prioress and some of her nuns were accused of gross immorality and squandering the convent's funds on hunting and extravagant entertaining. All that remains today of the priory is the much restored parish church that was the priory church. Another interesting building here is Budgenor Lodge which, when it was built in 1793, was a model workhouse and as such was much admired by visiting dignitaries.

FERNHURST
MAP 1 REF C4

4½ miles N of Midhurst on the A286

Just to the east of this pretty village, with its assorted tile hung cottages surrounding the village green, lies **Black Down**, rising abruptly from the Sussex Weald. A sandstone hill covered in heather, gorse and silver birch, that is an ideal environment for a variety of upland birdlife, the summit is the highest point in Sussex and from here there are views over the Weald and South Downs to the English Channel.

A particularly fine viewpoint, known as the **Temple of the Winds**, lies on the southern crest and one of the footpaths up the hill has been named locally as **Tennyson's Lane**, after the famous poet who lived for 20 years in the area. At one time a Royal navy signal tower stood on Tally Knob, a prominent outcrop to the southeast of the Temple of the Winds. A development of the tried and tested system of fire beacons, in 1796 the Admiralty introduced the Shutter Telegraph here as a more sophisticated means of passing messages between Portsmouth and London. Though ingenious, the system was found to be impractical and was soon abandoned.

To the west of Fernhurst, in the late 12th century, an Augustinian priory, on an altogether less grand scale then the magnificent Michelham Priory which lies near Upper Dicker, was founded. At the time of the Dissolution the priory became a farmhouse and one of the first floor rooms, which was originally the prior's chamber, is decorated with Tudor murals.

LURGASHALL
MAP 1 REF C4

4½ miles NE of Midhurst off the A283

This delightful rural village has, as a backdrop, the wooded slopes of Black Down, where Tennyson lived at **Aldworth House**. The village's largely Saxon church has an unusual loggia, or porch, outside where those who had travelled from afar could eat and rest before or after the service.

LODSWORTH
MAP 1 REF C4

2½ miles E of Midhurst off the A272

Situated on the River Lod, a small tributary of the River Rother, this old community has some fine buildings including a 13th century manor house and an early 18th century Dower House. The whitewashed village Church of St Peter lies on the outskirts of Lodsworth and, just to the north, is **St Peter's Well**, the water of which is supposed to have healing qualities.

TILLINGTON

MAP 1 REF C4

5 miles E of Midhurst on the A272

Dating back to the days before the Norman Conquest - the village appeared in the Domesday Book as Tolinstone - Tillington lies beside the western walls of Petworth House. The local landmark here, however, is **All Hallows' Church** and, in particular, its tower. Built in 1810, the tower is topped by stone pinnacles and a crown that is very reminiscent of the lower stage of the Eiffel Tower. Known as a Scots Crown, the church and its tower have featured in paintings by both Turner and Constable.

DUNCTON

MAP 1 REF C4

5 miles SE of Midhurst on the A285

Sheltered beneath Duncton Hill, beside Burton Park, the main building of St Michael's Girls' School, stands a small church on the wall of which can be seen the Royal Arms of Charles I dated 1636.

Found at the foot of the South Downs and surrounded by two acres of woodland gardens, **Wild Cherries** is a truly hidden place. An attractive and modern chalet style bungalow built in the early 1970s, this is the home of Sue and Martin Dadswell who offer excellent bed and breakfast accommodation in a choice of three guest rooms - two of which are on the ground floor. Each of the rooms is tastefully decorated and furnished to the same high standard as the rest of the bungalow and from all the windows there are glorious views over the grounds. Sue serves a delicious breakfast each morning in the conservatory

Wild Cherries, Dyehouse Lane, Duncton, near Petworth, West Sussex GU28 0LF Tel: 01798 342313

overlooking the surrounding countryside and guests are made to feel members of the family. From the garden, which also contains a trout stream, there are walks directly to the uplands, Downs and pubs. An ideal holiday base for family as both children and dogs are welcome, Sue has an unlimited supply of information about the surrounding area, including places of interest and good pubs and restaurants, and is sure to help make everyone's holiday as complete as possible. Wild Cherries is ETB listed Commended.

CHARLTON
MAP 1 REF C5

5½ miles S of Midhurst off the A286

The village is the home of the first regular fox hunt in England, the famous Charlton Hunt, and the reason that the 1ST Duke of Richmond made his home at Goodwood House. The family maintained their links with the hunt and the Charlton made the 2ND Duke its master.

SINGLETON
MAP 1 REF C5

5½ miles S of Midhurst on the A286

Lying in the folds of the South Downs, in the valley of the River Lavant, prior to the Norman invasion, this was one of the largest and wealthiest manors in England and it was owned by Earl Godwin of Wessex, father of King Harold. Little remains here from Saxon times, except an ancient barn on the village green, though the **13TH century church** was built on the foundations of its Saxon predecessor. Inside the church, in the south aisle, is a memorial to Thomas Johnson, a huntsman of the nearby Charlton Hunt who died in 1744. There are also two interesting monuments to two successive Earls of Arundel who died within two years of each other in the mid 16TH century.

Singleton is also the home of the famous **Weald and Downland Open Air Museum,** an exemplary museum with over 40 reconstructed historic rural build-

Weald and Downland Open Air Museum, Singleton, near Chichester, West Sussex PO18 0EU Tel: 01243 811348 Fax: 01243 811475 website: www.wealddown.co.uk

ings from all over southeast England. Founded in 1971 by JR Armstrong, the museum's buildings were all at one time under threat of demolition, before being transported here.

The buildings vividly demonstrate the homes and workplaces of the past and include Titchfield's former Tudor market hall, farmhouses and agricultural buildings from the 15th and 16th centuries, a Victorian tollhouse from Bramber, a schoolroom from West Wittering, a working blacksmith's forge and the watermill from Lurgashall which produces flour everyday for sale in the shop and use in the lakeside café. Several interiors have been furnished as they may have been during the building's heyday and visitors can take a look at the Tudor farmstead, with its fireplace in the middle of the hall, traditional farmyard animals and gardens, and the Victorian schoolroom is complete with blackboard, benches and school bell. To complement the buildings, five historic gardens have been carefully researched and planted, using traditional methods, to demonstrate the changes and continuities in ordinary gardens from 1430-1900.

This enchanting and unusual collection is situated in a delightful 50 acre park on the southern edge of the village. The museum also arranges demonstrations of rural skills and children's activities' days where traditional games, trades and crafts of the past, such as basket making and bricklaying, can be enjoyed. Finally, after taking in the many different experiences this atmospheric museum has to offer, enjoy a simple tasty meal in a medieval hall or picnic in the open. Relax and delight in this fabulous landscape.

WEST DEAN
MAP 1 REF C5
6 miles S of Midhurst on the A286

Just to the south of this pretty community of flint cottages, the land rises towards the ancient hilltop site known as **The Trundle**. One of the four main Neolithic settlements in Sussex, the large site was fortified during the Iron Age, when massive circular earth ramparts and a dry ditch were constructed. Named after the Old English for wheel, the site now enjoys fine views over Chichester, Singleton and Goodwood Racecourse.

The Selsey Arms, a handsome and welcoming free house on the main road in the village, is an excellent place to stop. Originally a much smaller Tudor building, it now incorporates the once derelict, now carefully restored, former village hall next door. The pretty, whitewashed stone and clapboard exterior is trimmed with hanging baskets of flowers. A colourful and informative collection of race cards adorns the surround of the public bar - on loan from a local jockey, a reminder of the area's connections with Goodwood. The dining area is intimate and cheerful. Apart from the traditional bar snacks, chef Kelly is a expert at staples such as homemade steak and kidney pie and farmhouse paté and toast as well as more adventurous cuisine such as broccoli and potato in cream cheese sauce, sweet and sour chicken stir fry and wheat casserole. Own-

**The Selsey Arms, West Dean, near Chichester,
West Sussex PO18 0QX Tel: 01243 811246**

ers Rod and Caroline Combes take great pride in and work very hard to achieve the standard of service on offer, and it shows.

Found amidst the rolling South Downs, **West Dean Gardens** immerses the visitor in a classic 19TH century designed landscape with its highly acclaimed restoration of the walled kitchen garden, the 16 original glasshouses and frames dating from the 1890s, the 35 acres of ornamental grounds, the 40 acres St Roche's arboretum and the extensive landscaped park. All the various areas of

**West Dean Gardens, West Dean, near Chichester,
West Sussex PO18 0QZ Tel: 01243 818210/811301**

this inspiring and diverse garden are linked by a scenic parkland walk. A particular feature of the grounds is the lavishly planted 300 foot Edwardian pergola, designed by Harold Peto, which acts as a host for a variety of climbers including roses, clematis and honeysuckle. Meanwhile, the beautifully restored Victorian glasshouses are home to vines, figs and soft fruits as well as an outstanding collection of chilli peppers, aubergines, tomatoes and extensive floral displays. Throughout the grounds there are also various summerhouses offering visitors not only shade but a peaceful setting in which to contemplate the views. The Visitor Centre, which overlooks the beautiful Lavant valley and West Dean Park, houses a quality licensed restaurant for refreshments ranging from morning coffee to lunches and luxury afternoon teas, whilst the Garden Shop has an imaginative range of gifts and plants for sale. Whether a garden fanatic or a casual visitor, staying an hour or all day, there is always something to enjoy at West Dean Gardens. The gardens are open daily from March to October and there are a series of events held throughout the year.

CHILGROVE
MAP 1 REF C5

6 miles SW of Midhurst on the B2141

Offering much more than bed and breakfast and yet not quite a hotel, **Forge Cottage** provides guests with every modern comfort in a charming and intimate setting. The building, a 17ᵗᴴ century blacksmith's cottage, surrounded by a large and attractive garden, lies at the heart of some of Sussex's most glorious

Forge Cottage, Chilgrove, Chichester, West Sussex PO18 9HX
Tel: 01243 535333 Fax: 01243 535363
e-mail: Forgecottage@btinternet.com

countryside and there are many lovely walks that can be taken straight from the grounds. The traditional brick and flint cottage has been lovingly restored by owner, Neil Rusbridger, who has played close attention to the building's original detail whilst also providing a homely and relaxing interior for all to enjoy. The guest accommodation comprises five delightful rooms, all of which have either ensuite or private bathrooms, and each of which is charmingly furnished and decorated in a pleasing and cosy manner and there are additional touches such as fresh flowers, mineral water and light snacks and morning tea available on room service. Neil, until recently chef and co-owner at the nearby highly acclaimed inn, also prepared suppers, taken with other guests or as room service, and dinner as a house party. Breakfast too is a splendid feast and, after a stay here, visitors will not be surprised to learn that Forge Cottage comes highly recommended by all the leading guide books.

To the north of this village, which is situated in a wooded valley, lies **Treyford Hill** where a line of five bell shaped barrows, known as the **Devil's Jump**, can be found. Dating back to the Bronze Age, these burial mounds - where the cremated remains of tribal leaders were interred in pottery urns - received their descriptive name as a result of the local superstitious habit of attributing unusual, natural features of the landscape to the work of the Devil.

WEST MARDEN   Map 1 ref B5
9 miles SW of Midhurst off the B2146

The largest of the four Marden hamlets that are all linked by quiet country lanes, West Marden is a picturesque place much loved by artists. It is, however, the only one of the four settlements without a church. **North Marden**, itself only a tiny place, is home to the Norman Church of St Mary which is one of the smallest in the county whilst, **Up Marden**'s minute 13th century church, which stands on the ancient Pilgrims' Way between Winchester and Chichester, is only a little bigger. Of the four Mardens, **East Marden**, is the most village like and, on the village green, there is a thatched well house with a notice reading, 'Rest and be Thankful but do not Wreck me'. As the well is still very much in existence, the advice has been heeded down the centuries.

Dating back to the 16th century and now a listed building, **The Victoria Inn** is a charming and delightful country inn. With a patio to the side that acts as a real sun trap during the summer and a large grassed beer garden with a tree house and swings for the children, the idyllic picture of the exterior is very much carried inside. Here, the full character of the building has been preserved through the years and, as well as the inglenook fireplace and exposed beams, pew seating and wooden floors add to the atmosphere of age and antiquity. However, The Victoria Inn is not just another country inn that has managed to escape the ravages of time as here visitors are treated to a wonderful menu of delicious dishes that range from bar food through to full à la carte. The regularly changing menus are prepared and presented by experienced chefs Tony

**The Victoria Inn, West Marden, near Chichester,
West Sussex PO18 9EN Tel: 01705 631722**

Merritt and Martin Robinson who, as partners, also own and manage the inn itself. Naturally, every dish is freshly prepared and cooked to order and fish and seafood, the house speciality, feature heavily in the menu. Visitors can either take advantage of the cosy non smoking dining room or take their meal in the bar whilst enjoying a drink from the excellent selection of wines and real ales on offer.

COMPTON
MAP 1 REF B5

8 miles SW of Midhurst on the B2146

A tranquil settlement of brick and flint buildings, Compton lies under the steep slope of **Telegraph Hill**. Close to the hill is a grassy mound which is, in fact, a Neolithic long barrow that is locally known as **Bevis' Thumb**. This mysterious burial site was named after a local giant, Bevis (the same Bevis who threw his sword from the battlements of Arundel Castle), who, as well as being very tall, had a weekly diet of an ox washed down with two hogsheads of beer.

SOUTH HARTING
MAP 1 REF B5

6 miles W of Midhurst on the B2146

One of the most attractive villages of the South Downs, South Harting not only has ancient thatched cottages but also more elegant red brick Georgian houses than its neighbours. The spire of the local church is, famously, covered in copper shingles, the bright verdigris hue of which can be seen from several miles away and acts as a signpost to this handsome place. Outside the church stand the ancient village stocks, along with a whipping post, and inside, there are several monuments including one commemorating the life of Sir Harry Fetherstonhaugh of Uppark.

Although the nearby grand house has seen many famous visitors, South Harting can boast of being the home of the novelist Anthony Trollope for the last two years of his life. Though here only a short time before his death in 1882, Trollope wrote four novels whilst in South Harting and his pen and paper knife can be seen in the church.

The village stands at the foot of **Harting Down**, beneath the steep scarp slope of the South Downs ridge, which is traversed by the South Downs Way. This spectacular long distance footpath and bridleway stretches for nearly 100 miles, from Winchester to Beachy Head and, here, the path skirts around **Beacon Hill**. At 793 feet above sea level, the hill is one of the highest points on the Downs and, surrounding the summit, is a rectangular Iron Age hillfort.

Just south of the village lies the magnificent house, **Uppark**, a National Trust property that is superbly situated on the crest of a hill. However, the climb up to the house was so steep that, when the house was offered to the Duke of Wellington after his victories in the Napoleonic Wars, he declined as he considered the drive to the mansion would require replacing his exhausted horses too many times. The house was built in the late 1680s for Lord Grey of Werke, one of the chief instigators of the Duke of Monmouth's rebellion of 1685 and also a hopeless cavalry commander who was taken prisoner at the battle of Sedgemoor. Lord Grey was let off with a fine and he retired from his none too illustrious military career and concentrated on building his house to the latest Dutch designs. As well as being a splendid house architecturally, the building of the house on this site was only made possible with the help of a water pump invented by Lord Grey's grandfather which brought water up to the hill top from a low lying spring.

It was a mid 18TH century owner, Sir Matthew Fetherstonhaugh, who created the lavish interiors by decorating and furnishing the rooms with rare carpets, elegant furniture and intriguing objects d'art. Dying in 1774, Sir Matthew left his estate to his 20 year old son, Sir Harry, who, with his great friend the Prince Regent, brought an altogether different atmosphere to the house. He installed his London mistress, Emma Hart (who later married Sir William Hamilton and became Lord Nelson's mistress), and carried on a life of gambling, racing and partying. However, in 1810, Sir Harry gave up his social life and, at the age of 70, he married his dairymaid, Mary Ann to the amazement and outrage of West Sussex society. He died, at the age of 92, in 1846 and both Mary Ann and then her sister Frances kept the house just as it had been during Sir Harry's life for a further 50 years.

This latter era of life at Uppark would have been remembered by the young HG Wells who spent a great deal of time here as his mother worked at the house. As well as exploring the grounds and gardens laid out by the early 19TH century designer Humphry Repton, Wells had a self taught education from Uppark's vast stock of books.

Unfortunately the upper floors of the house were destroyed by fire in 1989 and, after one of the National Trust's most extensive restoration programmes, the house was reopened to the public in 1995. Luckily, most of the house's 18TH century treasures were rescued from the fire and, as well as having been returned to its former splendour, the fine pictures, furniture and ceramics are now on view again in their original settings.

Also close to South Harting lies the site of the now demolished **Durford Abbey** - an isolated monastery founded in the 12TH century by a community of Premonstratensian monks, a strict vegetarian order founded in 1120 by St Norbert at Premontre, France. Unlike other orders of their time, which grew wealthy on the income from their monastic estates, life at Durford seems to have been very much a struggle for survival. In fact, so harsh was the monks' existence here that, on the monasteries dissolution in the 16TH century, is was described by a commissioner as 'The poorest abbey I have seen, far in debt and in decay.' Although little of the abbey remains today, the monks of Durford succeeded in leaving an important legacy in the form of two 15TH century bridges over the River Rother and its tributaries. (During the medieval period it was a duty of religious houses to provide and maintain such bridges.) Both Maidenmarsh Bridge, near the abbey site, and Habin Bridge, to the south of Rogate, are worth a visit and the latter, which consists of four semicircular arches, still carries the road to South Harting.

TROTTON   MAP 1 REF C4
3 miles W of Midhurst on the A272

This pleasant village lies in the broad valley of the River Rother to the west of Midhurst that was once a densely wooded area known for its timber and charcoal. The impressive **medieval bridge** in the village dates back to the 14TH century and, still carrying modern day traffic, the money for the bridge was given by Lord Camoys, who accompanied Henry V to Agincourt. Inside the **parish church** is a memorial to Lord Camoys, who died in 1419, and his second wife, Elizabeth Mortimer, who was the widow of Sir Henry 'Harry Hotspur' Percy. Here, too, can be found the oldest known memorial to a woman: a floor brass of Margaret de Camoys who died in around 1310.

PULBOROUGH

This ancient settlement has grown up close to the confluence of the Rivers Arun and Rother and it lies on the old Roman thoroughfare, Stane Street. Originally a staging post along the old route between London and Chichester, although Pulborough has a strategically important location near the rivers it was never developed like its rivals over the centuries. It remains today a pleasant and sizeable village that is well known for its freshwater fishing. The centre of Pulborough, on the old Roman route, is now a conservation area with several fine Georgian cottages clustered around the parish church which occupies a commanding hilltop position.

Just southeast of the village lies the **RSPB Pulborough Brooks Nature Reserve** where there is a nature trail through tree lined lanes that lead to views overlooking the restored wet meadows of the Arun Valley.

Built during the reign of Queen Anne and situated on a sandstone ridge overlooking the Arun valley and the South Downs, **Chequers Hotel** is a charming and delightful place that offers top quality hospitality in splendid surroundings. Owned and personally run by husband and wife, Martin and Pandora Pellett, this historic hotel offers a warm welcome to all visitors. Small and intimate, where guests can be assured of personal attention at all times, this wonderful hotel has been tastefully furnished and decorated throughout to a very high standard without loosing any of the building's original features that provide so much charm and character. As well as the 11 well appointed guest rooms, one of which has a four poster bed, guests will find that the public rooms, including the relaxing residents' lounge, make a peaceful haven in a busy world. The food at Chequers Hotel is also exceptional and well worth making the effort to seek out. Whilst the bright and airy conservatory coffee

Chequers Hotel, Old Rectory Lane, Pulborough,
West Sussex RH20 1AD Tel: 01798 872486 Fax: 01798 872715

shop serves light meals and snacks throughout the day, the elegant restaurant is the place for a marvellous evening meal. The interesting and mouthwatering menus change daily, but the standard of cuisine remains constant, and, with imaginative use made of local and seasonal meat, fish and vegetables, dining here is a delightful and exciting experience.

AROUND PULBOROUGH

WISBOROUGH GREEN
MAP 1 REF D4

5½ miles N of Pulborough on the A272

This pretty Sussex village has a large rectangular green, surrounded by horse chestnut trees, around which stand half timbered and tile hung cottages and houses. Nearby, the village **church of St Peter ad Vincula** is particularly interesting as the original Norman building, to which the 13ᵀᴴ century chancel was added, has walls that are almost five feet thick and a doorway that is 13 feet high! The suggestion is that this was an Anglo Saxon keep that was later enlarged into a church as the doorway is tall enough to admit a man on horseback. During the Middle Ages, this curious church was the centre of a pilgrimage as it contained several relics including the hair shirt, comb and bones of St James and a crucifix with a drop of the Virgin's milk set in crystal.

The village is set in the undulating country of the Weald and, to the west of Wisborough Green, there are two areas of preserved woodland which give an indication to today's visitors of how most of the land north of the Downs would have looked many thousands of years ago. Looking at the countryside now it is hard to imagine that, in the 16ᵀᴴ and 17ᵀᴴ centuries, this area was an important industrial centre. Thanks to the seemingly limitless supply of trees for fuel, iron foundries and forges prospered here right up until the time of the Industrial Revolution. A plentiful supply of high quality sand from the coast also led to a number of early glassworks being set up in the area. During the 16ᵀᴴ century, Huguenot settlers from France and the Low Countries introduced new and improved methods of glass manufacture and the industry flourished until the early 17ᵀᴴ century when lobbying by shipbuilders and iron smelters led to legislation banning the glassmakers from using timber to fire their furnaces.

'A lovely pub in a timeless village' is how **The Three Crowns** has been described - situated next to the 11ᵀᴴ century village Church of St Peter ad Vincula and the village pond on one side, and on the other, the village green where cricket is still played in the summer and the occasional hot air balloon will take off. Dating from the 15ᵀᴴ century, this building became the village pub in 1839 but not before it had served as the local law court in the 18ᵀᴴ century. Now very much a part of village life here, owners, Brian and Sandie Yeo, have made this just the place to make for if a quiet drink and good conversation are needed. A

The Three Crowns, Wisborough Green, near Billingshurst, West Sussex RH14 0DX Tel: 01403 700207

popular and well known meeting point, The Three Crowns has all the character and charm of an old village inn: there are wood blocked floors, beamed ceilings, comfortable seats, a mass of photographs of old Wisborough Green adorning the walls and a couple of resident ghosts!

The Three Crowns has an enviable reputation for the high standard of its cuisine. The tasty array of dishes, served at both lunchtime and evening, is homecooked by the resident chef, and offers a delicious selection of dishes that include traditional favourites such as steak, kidney and mushroom pie with shortcrust pastry, prime Scotch steaks and hugely popular mixed grill all supplied by a fine local butcher. The blackboard menu, which features such delights as slow roasted leg of lamb with creamy onion sauce and duck breasts with a delicious redcurrant and ginger sauce are served with a delicious selection of fresh vegetables and choice of potatoes. A wide choice of bar snacks, including freshly filled baguettes, jacket potatoes, authentic curries and pasta dishes can also be enjoyed in the lovely, large beer garden, which features the original village pond, patio, rose beds and lawned seating area. Excellent real ales, including Ballards Brewery ales who are based at nearby Midhurst, are kept in perfect condition.

For a unique fun day out for all the family **Fishers Farm Park** is a must that is sure to satisfy even the most demanding of children. Bringing together the delights of the rural farmyard with the excitement of dynamic adventure playgrounds and rides, this park caters for everyone from toddlers to grandparents. As well as the combine harvester and ponies rides, there is a whole assortment of animals to meet ranging from giant shire horses to goats, lambs and rabbits. Beside the 'beach area', which not only provides a safe place for toddlers to paddle but also adults to relax, are the adventure play areas with a whole host of imaginative swings, slides, and climbing frames that have all been constructed with safety in mind. For those who seek more mechanical diversions there is a merry-go-round from the 1950s and up-to-the-minute go-karts. As the children

**Fishers Farm Park, Newpound Lane, Wisborough Green, near
Billinghurst, West Sussex RH14 0EG Tel: 01403 700063
Fax: 01403 700823 e-mail: fishersfp@aol.com
website: fishersfarmpark.co.uk**

rush around taking in all the sights and sounds, those who like to take life at a
more leisurely pace can stop a while for a cup of tea and homemade cake or
lunch in the licensed restaurant. Finally, this is a day out that the weather
cannot spoil as there are several in-door play barns offering just as much fun and
excitement.

KIRDFORD
MAP 1 REF D4

5½ miles N of Pulborough off the A272

This large village, with its square green surrounded by stone cottages and tree-
lined main street, has more the feel of a small town. Like its neighbour,
Wisborough Green, Kirdford was also a centre for glassmaking - carried out here
between 1300 and 1600 - and the village sign incorporates diamonds of locally
made glass. Iron smelting also prospered here for 100 years from the mid 16TH
century and this accounts for the rather lavish extensions to the village's original Norman church.

LOXWOOD
MAP 1 REF D4

8 miles N of Pulborough on the B2133

This pleasant village, which lies off the beaten track and close to the county
border with Surrey, is on the **Wey and Arun Junction Canal** which opened in
1816 and linked London with the south coast. Like most British canals, the
coming of the railways saw an end to the commercial usefulness of these inland
waterways and, in 1871, it was closed. However, certain stretches have been
restored and as well as cruising along one of the country's most attractive canals
there are opportunities for strolling along the peaceful towpaths.

The village is also associated with the Christian Dependants, a religious sect
founded by preacher, John Sirgood, in the 1850s. The group were nicknamed

the 'Cokelers' because of their preference for cocoa over alcohol and their chapel and burial ground can be seen in Spy Lane.

WEST CHILTINGTON
MAP 1 REF D5
3 miles E of Pulborough off the A283

Built around a crossroads in the twisting lanes of the Wealdean countryside, this neat and compact village centres on the village green which is dominated by the delightful and relatively unrestored **Church of St Mary**. Famous for its medieval wall paintings that were only discovered in 1882, this charming Norman church has an oak shingled spire and a roof of Horsham stone. Beside the churchyard gate are the old village stocks and whipping post.

COOTHAM
MAP 1 REF D5
3 miles SE of Pulborough on the A283

The village is synonymous with **Parham**, the most westernmost and the grandest of the Elizabethan mansions that were built below the northern slopes of the Downs. Just west of the village and surrounded by a great deer park, the estate, in medieval times belonged to the Abbey of Westminster and, at the Dissolution of the Monasteries, passed into the hands of the Palmer family. As was customary, the foundation stone of the great mansion was laid by a child - Thomas Palmer - in 1577. The grandson and heir to the estate, Thomas did not fair as well as the house and he died of smallpox in 1605 after having served

Parham, nr Cootham

with both Drake and Hawkins. In the meantime, the splendid though rather dour grey stone building was constructed and, although it appears E shaped from the front, this Elizabethan mansion is actually in the form of an H as the wings project both north and south.

In 1601, Thomas Bysshop, a London lawyer, bought the estate and, for the next 300 years, it remained with that family. In 1922, the house and park was purchased by a son of Viscount Cowdray, Clive Pearson and, in 1948, after it had been used to house evacuees during World War II the present owners opened the property to the public. The splendid Elizabethan interiors have been restored to their former glory, including the magnificent 160 foot Long Gallery, Great Hall and Great Parlour, and an exceptional collection of period furniture, oriental carpets, rare needlework and fine paintings are on show.

The gardens too have been restored and the seven acres of wooded parkland contain a walled garden with herb beds and a Wendy House, greenhouses where plants and flowers are grown for the house, a lake and a statue garden. The house and gardens are open to the public between April and October.

Originally built as a coaching inn in the 17ᵀᴴ century, the traditional black and white timber framed frontage of **The Crown** makes it hard to miss once in the village. The adjacent Crown Cottages were once the inn's stables and it is alleged that they were also used by smugglers, of whom there are many tales in this area. However, today, life at The Crown, under the management of licensees Gill and Geoff Venn, is somewhat tamer. Attracting a pleasant mix of local people and walkers along the South Down Way, this is a warm and friendly

**The Crown, Pulborough Road, Cootham, West Sussex RH20 4JN
Tel: 01903 742625 Fax: 01903 740829**

family pub. The low ceilings, exposed beams and large inglenook fireplace all add to the charm of the inn and the addition of comfortable seating and fresh flowers gives a pleasant atmosphere in which to relax. As well as a good variety of real ales, lagers and beers behind the bar, the inn is well known for the delicious homecooked meals that are served throughout the week. With plenty of outdoor facilities for children, there are swings, a slide and an assault course, this is the perfect family inn.

STORRINGTON
3½ miles SE of Pulborough on the A283

MAP 1 REF D5

This old market town has a jumble of architectural styles from its small heavily restored Saxon church through to the 20TH century modern concrete buildings. However, from Storrington there is good access to the **South Downs Way** long distance footpath via Kithurst Hill. It was this beautiful surrounding countryside that inspired Francis Thompson to write his poem *Daisy* whilst he was staying in a local monastery and the composer, Arnold Bax, also lived in the area between 1940-51.

Back in the town, the heavily restored **Church of St Mary** has, inside, a Saxon stone coffin on which is the marble effigy of a knight who is thought to have been a crusader. When the author Dr AJ Cronin moved to the old rectory in the 1930s he used this legend as the basis for his novel *The Crusaders*.

Ideally situated for the towns of Worthing, Brighton and Chichester, **Greenacres Country Holidays** also offers visitors to Sussex the perfect opportunity to get away from it all. Set in glorious countryside, the selfcatering cottage units provide visitors with a peaceful and relaxing holiday base. Each of the chalets - there are two styles of unit, one for families and the other aimed at adults - has its own private garden whilst there is a heated swimming pool on

Greenacres Country Holidays, Greenacres, Washington Road, Storrington, West Sussex RH20 4AF Tel: 01903 742538

the site. Everything needed for a successful holiday is provided in these well appointed chalets and there is even a complementary welcome pack of basic food supplies awaiting each new visitor. As both children and well behaved dogs are also very welcome here, the whole family can enjoy a holiday in these delightful and comfortable chalets. Cooks too can have a break as bed and breakfast accommodation is also available.

SULLINGTON
4½ miles SE of Pulborough off the A283

MAP 1 REF D5

This hamlet is home to a 115 foot **long barn** which rivals many tithe barns that were such a feature of the medieval monastic estate. An exceptional building with a braced tie beam roof, the barn, which is privately owned, can be viewed by appointment. Just outside Sullington is **Sullington Warren** - owned by the National Trust this expanse of open heathland was once used for farming rabbits and it now offers superb views across the South Downs.

AMBERLEY
MAP 1 REF D5

4 miles S of Pulborough on the B2139

An attractive village of thatched cottages situated above the River Arun, whose name means 'fields yellow with buttercups', Amberley is an ancient place whose history goes back to the days of the Saxons. Lands in this area were granted to St Wilfrid by King Cedwalla in around AD 680 and the village church of today is thought to stand on the foundations of a Saxon building constructed by St Wilfrid, the missionary who converted the South Saxons to Christianity. Later, in the 12TH century, Bishop Luffa of Chichester rebuilt the church and it still has a strong Norman appearance.

At around the same time as the church was being rebuilt, a fortified summer palace for the Bishops of Chichester was also constructed. During the late 14TH century, when there was a large threat of a French sea invasion, Bishop Rede of Chichester enlarged the summer palace and added a great curtain wall in order to protect the north side of the Arun Valley. Still more a manor house than a true castle, **Amberley Castle** is said to have offered protection to Charles II during his flight to France in 1651. Today, it is privately owned.

During the 18TH and 19TH centuries, chalk was quarried from Amberley and taken to the many lime kilns in the area. Later, large quantities of chalk were needed to supply a new industrial process which involved the high temperature firing of chalk with small amounts of clay to produce Portland cement. Situated just to the south of Amberley and on the site of an old chalk pit and limeworks is **Amberley Museum**, which concentrates on the industry of this area. Very much a working museum, which occupies a site of 36 acres, visitors can ride the length of the museum on a workman's train as well as view the comprehensive collection of narrow gauge engines, from steam to electric. The history of roads and roadmaking is also explored and, in the Electricity Hall, there are an amazing as-

Amberley Museum

sortment of electrical items from domestic appliances to generating and supply equipment. Meanwhile, in the workshop section, there are all manner of tradesmen's shops including a blacksmith's, pottery, boatbuilder's and a printing works.

Leaving industry aside, to the north of Amberley there are a series of water meadows known as the **Amberley Wild Brooks**. Often flooded and inaccessible by car, this 30 acre conservation area and nature reserve is a haven for bird, animal and plant life. The trains running on the Arun Valley line cross the meadows on specially constructed embankments which were considered wonders of modern engineering when the line was first opened in 1863.

HARDHAM
MAP 1 REF D5

1 mile SW of Pulborough on the A29

This tiny hamlet, on the banks of the River Arun, is home to the Saxon **Church of St Botolph** which is famous for its medieval wall paintings. Considered some of the finest in England, the oldest of the paintings dates from around 1100 and among the scenes on view are images of St George slaying the dragon and the Serpent tempting Adam and Eve. The murals are thought to have been worked by a team of artists based at St Pancras Priory in Lewes and they were also responsible for the paintings at Coombes and Clayton.

At one time Hardham had a small Augustinian monastic house and the site of **Hardham Priory** can be found just south of the hamlet. Now a farmhouse, the priory's cloisters have been incorporated into a flower garden. From the site a footpath leads to the disused **Hardham Tunnel**, a channel which was built to provide a short cut for river barges wishing to avoid an eastern loop of the River Arun.

BIGNOR
MAP 1 REF D5

5 miles SW of Pulborough off the A29

The main thoroughfares of this pretty village are arranged in an uneven square and, as well as a photogenic 15th century shop, there are some charming ancient domestic buildings to be seen. In 1811, a ploughman working on the east side of the village unearthed a **Roman Mosaic Floor** which, when further excavations were carried out, proved to be part of a villa built at the end of the 2nd century AD. One of the largest sites in Britain - there are some 70 Roman buildings here surrounding a central courtyard - it is thought that the find was the administration centre of a large agricultural estate. The villa, being the home of a wealthy agricultural master, was extended throughout the time of the Roman occupation and the mosaic decoration of the house is some of the finest to be seen in this country.

Unlike the Roman excavations at Fishbourne, this remains a relatively undiscovered site for tourists and, charmingly, the exposed remains are covered, not by modern day structures, but by the thatched huts that were first built to protect them in 1814. The 80 foot long mosaic along the north corridor is the longest on display in Britain and among the characters depicted on the mosaics are Venus, Medusa and an array of Gladiators. The **Museum** here not only houses a collection of artefacts revealed during the excavation work but there is also a display on the history of the Roman settlement and its underfloor heating system or hypocaust.

FITTLEWORTH

MAP 1 REF D5

2½ miles W of Pulborough on the A283

An acknowledged Sussex beauty spot, the village, though now on the main Pulborough to Petworth road, has retained much of its charm which has drawn people here over the years. Well known amongst fishermen, this is still a great place for the sport on either the River Rother or, further downstream, where it joins the River Arun. Others drawn here have been artists, many of whom stayed at the village inn. However, found in the middle of woodlands is **Brinkwells**, a thatched cottage and the home of the village's most famous visitor, the composer Edward Elgar. First coming here in 1917, when he wrote his famous cello concerto, Elgar returned for the last time in 1921. Appropriately, the Jubilee clock in the village church has a very musical chime.

Here in this secluded and picturesque village setting, **The Swan Inn** is a charming and traditional rural hotel surrounded by forests and hills, with the South Downs Way for a backdrop. Handy for the business and leisure traveller

The Swan Inn, Lower Street, Fittleworth, West Sussex RH20 1EN
Tel: 01798 865429 Fax: 01798 865721

- Gatwick and Southampton airports are less than an hour away, the railway station at Pulborough only two miles away, Arundel eight miles distant and the centres of Horsham and Chichester 15 miles off - the Swan combines the best in traditional coaching inn standards with modern facilities usually associated with much larger establishments. The stately building dates back to 1382; the interior with its open log fires and exposed oak beamed ceilings, is welcoming and peaceful. Here, an informal and relaxed atmosphere goes hand in hand with first class service. There are 11 tastefully furnished guest bedrooms, two with four poster beds. In the Picture Room, 33 original works of art, each one painted in situ and extremely valuable, grace the walls. In the cosy oak beamed restaurant, hearty breakfasts, lunches, tempting evening meals and light suppers are served with style.

STOPHAM   Map 1 ref D5
1 mile NW of Pulborough off the A283

This charming place, where a handful of cottages cluster around the early Norman church, lies on the banks of the River Rother. The family home of the Barttelot family, who can trace their ancestry back to the Norman invasion, **Stopham House** is still here as is the splendid early 15TH century bridge which the family were instrumental in constructing. The impressive **Stopham Bridge** is widely regarded as the finest of its kind in Sussex and, though the tall central arch was rebuilt in 1822 to allow masted vessels to pass upstream towards the Wey and Arun Canal, the medieval structure is coping well with today's traffic without a great deal of modern intervention.

Found adjacent to the village's famous old bridge, the history of **The White Hart** is very much intertwined with that of Stopham. The building has been

The White Hart, Stopham Bridge, near Pulborough,
West Sussex RH20 1DS Tel: 01798 873321

here since the 13TH century, though it did not become an inn until the 1500s, but every since it has been serving the needs of both locals and travellers on this once busy main road. However, the inn has seen many changes over the years and, today, though it has retained all its old world charm and character, there is much more to The White Hart than just a good pint of beer that is still served in the traditional country inn bar. From the early 1980s, the inn has been gaining a reputation for the excellence of its cuisine and this is an area that the present landlords, Chris and Tereza Maddocks, have built upon since taking over in the summer of 1999. The Bistro, the inn's separate rustic dining area is small and intimate and the ideal place to enjoy the superb homecooked dishes on offer. Very much specialising in fish, there are eight different dishes to choose from each day, the menu also includes traditional pub favourites and Dreister Toft (a German meat stew) that is prepared by Chris. Finally, as well as the delightful riverside setting, The White Hart also hosts unusual events, including theatrical productions, in the small theatre in the inn's garden.

PETWORTH
MAP 1 REF D4
5 miles NW of Pulborough on the A283

This historic town, though now a major road junction, still has many elements of an ancient feudal settlement - the old centre, a great house and a wall dividing the two. Mentioned in the Domesday Book, where it appeared as *Peteorde*, this was a market town and the square is thought to have originated in the 13TH century and its street fair dates back to 1189. Between the 14TH and the 16TH

centuries this was an important cloth weaving centre and a number of fine merchants' and landowners' houses remain from those days, including **Daintrey House** which though its has a Georgian front façade has Elizabethan features to the rear. Another house, **Leconfield Hall**, dates from 1794 and, before becoming a public hall, it was the courthouse and council meeting place. Meanwhile, the garden of **Lancaster House**, close by, is said to have been used as a hiding place for the church silver during the time of Cromwell.

Petworth

As well as taking time to wander the streets here and see the many interesting houses, cottages and other buildings, visitors should make time to also take in the town's two museums. The **Petworth Cottage Museum** is housed in a 17th century cottage of the Leconfield estate and that has been restored to the days of 1910 when it was the home of Maria Cummings. A seamstress at nearby Petworth House and a widow with four grown up children, the cottage recreates the domestic setting in which she lived and includes her sewing room.

The unusual **Doll House Museum** has an interesting collection of over 100 doll's houses, inhabited by 2000 miniature people, that have been put together to create an image of present day life. Among the one twelfth size houses there are replicas of the Royal Albert Hall, a prison and a museum full of tourists.

However, what brings most visitors to Petworth is the grand estate of **Petworth House** that is now in the hands of the National Trust. Built between 1688 and 1696, on the site of a medieval manor house belonging to the Percy family by Charles Seymour, the 6th Duke of Somerset, Petworth House is a simple and elegant building that has more the look of a French château than an English country house and both French and English architects have been suggested. The construction of the house was completed by the Duke's descendant, the 2nd Earl of Egremont, and it was he who had the grounds and deer park landscaped by Capability Brown in 1752.

Today, the house is home to one of the finest art collections outside London and the interior design, where one room leads directly into another, lends itself perfectly to life as an art gallery. Amongst the works on view are paintings by Rembrandt, Van Dyck, Holbein, Reynolds, Gainsborough and Turner, who was a frequent visitor to Petworth House. On a less grand scale, in decoration terms, the servants' block is also open to the public and provides an interesting insight into life below stairs.

Just south of the estate is the **Coultershaw Water Wheel and Beam Pump**, one of the earliest pumped water systems that was installed in 1790 to pipe water two miles to Petworth House.

EBERNOE   Map 1 ref D4
4 miles N of Petworth off the A283

Found near Petworth in the heart of West Sussex and close to unspoilt woodland, **Butcherland Farm** has been in Ivan Wadey's family for many years - in fact, Ivan was born here. Dating back to the 16th century, the farmhouse is a wonderful old building surrounded by a peaceful and secluded garden with the farmland beyond. From this large attractive home, Ivan and his wife, Margaret, offer excellent bed and breakfast accommodation in a choice of three guest rooms. Each room has a separate bathroom and views over the garden as well as providing guests with a comfortable and relaxing place in which to rest. Guests also have their own well furnished lounge, complete with open fire, television and a whole host of local guide books, and even a kitchenette though

**Butcherland Farm, Ebernoe, near Petworth, West Sussex GU28 9JX
Tel & Fax: 01403 820251**

there is no need to prepare breakfast as a delicious homecooked meal is served to guests each morning. Ideal for all the family, not only can guests freely wander around the garden, enjoy relaxing on the patio area, make friends with the farm's two miniature Shetland ponies but there is also coarse fishing available in the farm's own ponds. One look at the remarks made by previous guests in the visitors' book shows that Butcherland Farm is well worth finding.

3 The West Sussex Weald

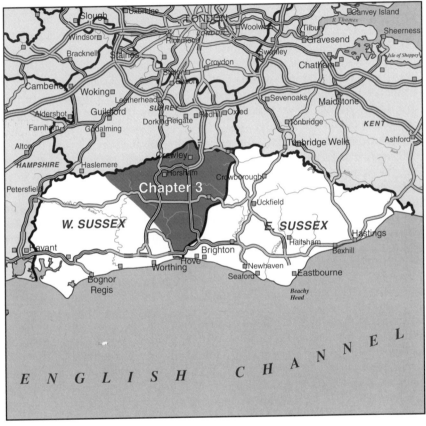

INTRODUCTION

This area, to the north of the South Downs, is called a Weald, a word that is derived from the German word Wald, meaning forest. This would suggest an area covered in woodland and, though some areas of the great forest remain, the landscape now is one of pastures enclosed by hedgerows. From the Middle Ages onwards, until the time of the Industrial Revolution, the area was very much associated with iron working, and less so, glassmaking. The trees were felled for fuel to drive the furnaces and streams were dammed to create hammer ponds. The legacy of this once prosperous industry can be seen in the wealth of elaborate buildings and, particularly, the splendid churches, that were built on the profits of the industry.

Those interested in visiting grand houses will find that this region of West Sussex has several to offer. Close to East Grinstead lies Standen, a remarkable Victorian country house that, now it has been restored to its original glory, is a wonderful example of the Arts and Crafts Movement. The low half timber 15th century house, the Priest House, at West Hoathly, was built as an estate office for the monks from St Pancras Priory, Lewes. Now restored it is open to the public as a museum filled with 18th and 19th century furniture. The magnificent Elizabeth mansion, Danny, at Hurstpierpoint, as a very special place in history as this is where Lloyd George and his war cabinet drew up the terms of the armistice to end World War I. In private hands today, the house is occasionally open to the public.

Near Ardingly lies Wakehurst Place, a striking Elizabethan mansion built by the Culpeper family in 1590. Now leased to the Royal Botanical Gardens at Kew, the magnificent collection of trees and shrubs in the grounds are a treat well worth seeing. Other great gardens can also be found in this region of West Sussex, including Leonardslee at Lower Beeding which was laid out in the late 19th century by Sir Edmund Loder and Hymans, which was created with the help of the 19th century gardening revivalists William Robinson and Gertrude Jekyll.

HORSHAM

This ancient town, which takes its name from a Saxon term meaning 'horse pasture', was founded in the mid 10th century. Some 300 years later, Horsham had grown into a prosperous borough and market town which was considered important enough to send two members to the new Parliament established in 1295. Between 1306 and 1830, Horsham, along with Lewes and Chichester, took it in turns to hold the county assizes. During the weeks the court was held in Horsham, large numbers of visitors descended on the town giving it a carnival atmosphere. Public executions were also held here, either on the common or on the Carfax, and these include one, in 1735, of a man who refused to speak at his trial. Sentenced to death by compression, three hundredweight of stones were placed on his chest for three days. When the man still refused to speak, the gaoler added his own weight to the man's chest and killed him outright. The **Carfax** today is a thriving pedestrianized shopping centre and nothing is left of the horrors of its past.

Horsham's architectural gem is **The Causeway**, a quiet tree lined street of old buildings that runs from the Georgian fronted town hall to the 12th century Church of St Mary, where can be found a simple tablet commemorating the life of Percy Bysshe Shelley, a celebrated local inhabitant. Here too can be found

Horsham

the gabled 16ᵀᴴ century **Causeway House** - rambling building it is now home to the **Horsham Museum**, a purpose for which its layout is ideal. This excellent museum has recreations of a Sussex farmhouse kitchen, a wheelwright's and saddler's shop, and a blacksmith's forge and, among the old prints and photographs, is an extraordinary drawing of a hard labour machine that was installed in Horsham Goal. It consisted of a long row of hand operated cranks, linked to a vast wind vane, which beat the air for no apparent purpose other than to exhaust the convicts. Concentrating on local history in particular, the collection is also varied and includes toys, costumes, 19ᵀᴴ century literature and aspects of town life.

Just two miles southwest of Horsham lies the famous **Christ's Hospital School**, a Bluecoat school that was founded in London in 1552 by Edward VI. The school moved to Horsham in 1902 and the present buildings incorporate some of the original London edifices. Bluecoat refers to the traditional long dark blue cloak that is still worn by the pupils though, today, the school takes both boys and girls.

AROUND HORSHAM

RUSPER   Map 2 ref E3
3 miles N of Horsham off the A264

This secluded village of tile hung and timbered cottages grew up around a 13ᵀᴴ century priory. However, all that remains today of Rusper Priory is the church where, in the churchyard, a prioress and four sisters are buried. Although the church has a medieval tower, this is all that is left of the original building as the rest was rebuilt in the mid 19ᵀᴴ century by the Broadwater family. The family's wealth came from their piano manufacturing business and Lucy Broadwater (who died in 1929), to whom there is a memorial tablet in the church, was a leading figure in the revival of English folk music.

GATWICK AIRPORT
Map 2 ref F3

7½ miles NE of Horsham off the A23

The airport opened to commercial air traffic in 1936 when the first passengers took off for Paris. The return fare was £4 5 shillings (£4.25) and this included the return first class railfare from Victoria Station, London to the airport. A month later the airport was officially opened by the Secretary of State for Air when he also opened the world's first circular air terminal here which was immediately christened the Beehive. During World War II, the airport, like all other British airports, was put under military control and, amongst other uses, it was one of the bases for the D-Day operations.

After the war, the terminal buildings were extended and, in 1958, the new airport was reopened. Amongst Gatwick Airport's other notable firsts was the pier leading from the terminal to the aircraft stands giving passengers direct access to the planes and Gatwick was the first airport in the world to combine air, rail and road travel under one roof. Further extensions have increased the airport's capacity to a point where, now, it can handle 30 million passengers a year flying to destinations right around the world.

Gatwick Airport Skyview gives visitors the chance to see behind the scenes of this busy airport through its multimedia theatre and there is also a real aircraft and cockpit to explore.

CRAWLEY
Map 2 ref EF

6½ miles NE of Horsham on the A23

A modern town, one of the original new towns created after the New Towns Act of 1946, Crawley is really an amalgamation of the villages of Three Bridges and Ifield with the small market town of Crawley. Though much has been lost under the new developments, Crawley probably dates back to Saxon times though it remained a quiet and unassuming place until the late 18ᵗʰ century. A convenient distance from both London and Brighton, it was used by the Prince Regent and his friends as a stopping over point as they commuted between the south coast resort of Brighton and the metropolis. However, the coming of the railways took away the need of a resting place and so Crawley returned to its quiet life. Fortunately, the aptly named **George Hotel**, a long low coaching inn, has survived and it can be found in what remains of the original centre of Crawley.

MANNINGS HEATH
Map 2 ref E4

2 miles SE of Horsham on the A281

Just north of the village lies **St Leonard's Forest**, one of the few wooded heathland areas to survive the long term ravages of the timber fuelled iron industry of the Weald. Rising in places to around 500 feet, the forest lies on the undulating sandstone ridge that is bounded by Horsham, Crawley and Handcross. According to local folklore, St Leonard's Forest is the home of the legendary nine foot dragon which roamed the heath and terrorised the surrounding villagers. Coincidentally, the bones of a prehistoric iguanodon have since been discovered in the forest by the Sussex based geologist, Dr Gideon Mantell.

Although today's **Dun Horse** was built in the 1920s, the original pub was an early 18th century coaching inn on the once busy London to Brighton route. However, the tradition of offering travellers excellent hospitality and a place to rest during their long and uncomfortable journey is very much alive and well here. A pleasant and relaxing place, The Dun Horse has several areas inside including a central bar, a dining area and a dedicated games room. Each provides ample space for enjoying a pint of one of the superb real ales here and also

The Dun Horse, Brighton Road, Mannings Heath, near Horsham, Sussex RH13 6HZ Tel: 01403 265783 Fax: 01403 270905

soaking up the real village pub atmosphere. As well as establishing a reputation for fine ales, landlady, Annette Christian, is keen to make the pub a place for all the family. The large garden to the rear of the building is ideal for children and here they can not only join in with the summer barbecues and play whilst their parents have a quiet drink on the patio but there are also guinea pigs and an aviary to keep them amused.

The area in which The Dun Horse does excel is in the kitchen. Head chef René Kosch is responsible for the imaginative menus that have put the pub on the dining out map of the county. A well respected chef and well known in the area, René originally comes from Germany and not only does he introduce dishes from his home country to the menu but there are several German themed evenings throughout the year. A great place that is well worth seeking out, The Dun Horse can also offer accommodation to visitors in a choice of three well appointed, ensuite guest rooms.

LOWER BEEDING
3 miles SE of Horsham on the B2110

MAP 2 REF E4

The name of the village, along with that of its near namesake, Upper Beeding to the south, is somewhat confusing. Lower Beeding is actually situated on the summit of a hill whilst Upper Beeding lies in one of the lowest parts of West Sussex. However, this can be explained by looking at the derivation of the shared name. Beeding is derived from the Old English 'Beadingas' which means 'Beada's people' and the Upper and Lower refer to the importance of, rather than the geographical positions of, the two settlements.

Just to the south of the village lies the beautiful **Leonardslee Gardens**, in a natural valley created by a tributary of the River Adur. Laid out by Sir Edmund Loder who began his task in 1889, the gardens are still maintained by the family and are world famous for their spring displays of azaleas, magnolias and rhododendrons that have been planted around the seven landscaped lakes. Deer and wallabies live in the semiwild habitat around the small lakes and whilst there are several miles of walks around this large area, there are also small gardens, including a bonsai garden to enjoy. The Loder family collection of motor vehicles which date from 1895 to 1900 is an interesting and informative display of the various different designs adopted by the earliest car constructors.

Leonardslee Gardens, Lower Beeding

COWFOLD
4 miles SE of Horsham on the A272

MAP 2 REF E4

This is a picturesque village of cottages clustered around the parish **Church of St Peter** that is home to one of the most famous brasses in Sussex. Dating back to the 15TH century, the life size brass is of Thomas Nelond, Prior of Lewes in the 1420s, and the brass, along with its elaborate canopy, is over 10 feet long.

Looking at Cowfold today it is hard to believe that is was once an important centre of the iron industry. The abundance of timber for fuel and reliable streams to drive the bellows and heavy hammers made this an active iron smelting area from medieval times through to the end of the 18TH century. In order to secure a steady supply of water to these early foundries, small rivers were dammed to form mill or hammer ponds and a number of disused examples can still be found in the surrounding area.

Just to the south of Cowfold and rising above the trees is the spire of **St Hugh's Charterhouse**, the only Carthusian monastery in Britain. Founded in the 1870s, after the order had been driven out of France, the 30 or so monks of this contemplative order live cut off from the rest of the world behind the high stone walls. Each monk has his own cell, or hermitage, that is complete with its own garden and workshop and the monks only emerge from their solitude for services and dinner on Sunday.

UPPER BEEDING
MAP 2 REF E5

13 miles S of Horsham off the A2037

A sprawling village of cottages along the banks of the River Adur, during the Middle Ages, Upper Beeding was the home of **Sele Priory**, a Benedictine religious house founded in the late 11TH century by William de Braose. Long since destroyed, the site of the priory is now occupied by a private house.

Though a quiet place today, in the early 19TH century an important turnpike road passed through Upper Beeding and the old village toll house, one of the last in the county to remain in service, is now an exhibit at the Weald and Downland Museum, Singleton.

BRAMBER
MAP 2 REF E5

13 miles S of Horsham on the A283

Visitors seeing Bramber for the first time will find it hard to imagine that this small, compact village was once a busy port on the River Adur estuary during Norman times but its demise came as the river silted up. The name Bramber is derived from the Saxon 'Brymmburh' meaning fortified hill and when, after being given land here by William the Conqueror, William de Braose built his castle on the steep hill above the village it was probably on the foundations of a previous Saxon stronghold. Completed in 1090, the castle comprised a gatehouse and a number of domestic buildings surrounded by a curtain wall. An important stronghold whilst the port was active, the castle was visited by both King John and Edward I. Having survived the Middle Ages, the castle did not survive the Civil War and, though first held by the Royalists, it was all but demolished by the Parliamentarians. Today, the stark remains of **Bramber Castle** can be seen on the hilltop and the site is owned by English Heritage.

During the 15TH century, the lands of the de Braose family were transferred to William Waynflete, the then Bishop of Winchester and founder of Magdalen College, Oxford. It was Waynflete who was responsible for constructing **St Mary's House**, in 1470, a striking medieval residence that was first built as a home for four monks who were bridge wardens of the important crossing here over the River Adur. Now a Grade I listed building, this is a classic half timbered dwelling with fine wood panelled rooms, Elizabethan trompe l'œil paintings and medieval shuttered windows. However, large though the building is, what remains today is only half of the original construction that also acted as a resting place for pilgrims travelling to Chichester or Canterbury.

Following the Dissolution of the Monasteries, the house came into private ownership and was refurbished as a comfortable residence for a well-to-do family. The Painted Room was decorated for a visit by Queen Elizabeth I in 1585 and the room in which Charles II rested before fleeing to Shoreham and then France is known as the King's Room. Lovingly restored and with charming topiary gardens, the house is the setting for the Sherlock Holmes story *The Musgrave Ritual* and it has also featured in the *Dr Who* television series.

Finally, before the Reform Act of 1832 swept away the rotten boroughs, this tiny constituency returned two members to Parliament. This was despite the fact that, at one time, Bramber only had 32 eligible voters! One member of Parliament who benefited from the unreformed system was William Wilberforce who was more or less awarded one of the Bramber seats in recognition of his campaigning work against slavery.

The oldest parts of **The Castle Inn** date back to the 16ᵗ century and it was probably built as two cottages. However, that was many years ago and since then this splendid and very distinctive building has seen many changes including the several extensions that give it a highly individual appearance. In the summer months The Castle Inn's exterior takes on a whole new look when

The Castle Inn, The Street, Bramber, Steyning, West Sussex BN44 3WE
Tel: 01903 812102 Fax: 01903 816711

window boxes and hanging baskets, filled to overflowing with colourful flowering plants, cover the front and side façades - not surprisingly when seen, these displays have gained the pub many awards. The interior of this typical English inn is equally pleasing and, as well as the comfortable bar area and lounge, there is a separate games room and a dining room. The real ales, beers, lagers and all the other usual drinks served from the bar are complemented by the traditional menu of homecooked pub food that can be taken in the bar or, more formally, in the dining room. The roast Sunday lunches are particularly popular and well worth taking the time to enjoy. Finally, hosts Dave and Chris Mitchell also offer delightful accommodation in a choice of eight ensuite guest rooms that match the same high standards as the rest of the inn.

STEYNING
13 miles S of Horsham off the A283

MAP 2 REF E5

This ancient market town, whose High Street follows closely the line of the South Downs that are hidden behind it, was founded in the 8TH century by St Cuthman. An early Celtic Christian, Cuthman travelled from Wessex eastwards pushing his invalid mother in a handcart. On reaching Saxon Steyning, the wheel on the handcart broke as they passed Penfolds Field and the nearby haymakers laughed and jeered as the old lady was thrown to the ground. St Cuthman cursed the field and the unhelpful haymakers, and the heavens are said to have opened and torrential rain poured and spoilt their labours. To this day, it is said to rain whenever Penfolds Field is being mown. St Cuthman took his calamity as a sign that he should settle here and he built a timber church where Ethelwulf, the father of King Alfred, is believed to have been buried.

By the late Saxon period Steyning had grown to become an important port on the then navigable River Adur and, as well as being a royal manor owned by Alfred the Great, it also had a Royal Mint. By 1100, the silting of the river had caused the harbour to close but, fortunately, the town was well established and could continue as a market place. Designated a conservation area, there are many buildings of architectural and historical interest in the town's ancient centre. There are several 14TH and 15TH century hall type houses as well as Wealden cottages but the most impressive building is the famous **Old Grammar School** which was built in the 15TH century as the home of a religious order. An excellent place to discover Steyning's past is at **Steyning Museum** in Church Street where there are exhibitions showing both the town's history and local prehistoric finds.

Steyning's close proximity to the **South Downs Way** and the **Downs Link** (a long distance bridleway which follows the course of the old railway line to Christ's Hospital near Horsham and on in to Surrey), makes this a lovely base for both walking and riding holidays.

WASHINGTON
Map 2 ref E5
12 miles S of Horsham off the A24

Standing at the northern end of the Findon Gap, an ancient pass through the South Downs, despite the American connotations, this village's name is derived from the Saxon for 'settlement of the family of Wassa'. A pretty place, with a varied assortment of buildings, Washington stands between the chalk downland and the sandstone Weald and it was at the early 19th century inn, The Frankland Arms, that Hilaire Belloc found a 'nectar brewed in the waxing of the moon and of that barley which Brutus brought hither in the first founding of this land'.

Just southeast of the village, and not far from the South Downs Way, lies one of Sussex's most striking landmarks - **Chanctonbury Ring**. An Iron Age hillfort, the site is marked by a clump of beech trees that were planted in 1760 by Charles Goring who inherited the hill along with Wiston Park. Unfortunately, many of the trees suffered during the October hurricane of 1987 but enough remain to make this an eyecatching sight on the horizon. Meanwhile, the part 16th and part 19th century mansion of **Wiston Park** is now leased by the Foreign Office and, though it is not open to the public, views of the house and the park can be seen from the road leading to village church.

The countryside around Chanctonbury Ring inspired the composer John Ireland who, towards the end of his life in the 1950s, bought **Rock Mill** which lies below the hill. A converted tower mill, a plaque on the wall records that Ireland lived the happiest years of his life here before his death in 1962.

SHIPLEY
Map 2 ref E4
6 miles S of Horsham off the A272

As well as its pretty 12th century village church, this pleasant village also features a small disused toll house and a distinctive hammer pond that, in the 16th century, would have supplied water to drive the bellows and mechanical hammers in the adjacent iron foundry. However, Shipley is perhaps best known for being the former home of the celebrated Sussex writer Hilaire Belloc. He lived at **King's Land**, a low rambling house on the outskirts of the village, from 1906 until his death in 1953 and, appropriately enough, as a lover of windmills, he had one at the bottom of his garden. Built in 1879, **Shipley Mill** is the only remaining working smock mill in Sussex and, whilst being the county's last, it is also the biggest. Open to the public on a limited basis, the mill was completely restored and returned to working order after the writer's death.

Belloc is not the only connection that Shipley has with the arts for the composer John Ireland is buried in the churchyard of the village's interesting church that was built by the Knights Templar in 1125. The poet and traveller, Wilfrid Scawen Blunt, also lived at Shipley where he entertained celebrities of the day including Oscar Wilde, William Morris and Winston Churchill.

DIAL POST
MAP 2 REF E5
7 miles S of Horsham on the A24

Just to the east of the village lie the stark ruins of medieval **Knepp Castle**, a fortification built by William de Braose of Bramber to defend the upper reaches of the River Adur. All that remains of the once impressive Norman keep is a solitary wall standing on top of a low mound which is surrounded by a now dry moat.

Here in this charming village lies **Honeybridge Park**, a handsome and picturesque caravan park in a lovely countryside setting which boasts excellent views and very good facilities. Located down a quiet, rural lane, this pleasant and spotless site is ideal for a quiet, relaxing holiday. Owners Valerie and Jeff Burrows have acquired the site and are working hard to offer more and more conveniences while maintaining the site's secluded and uncrowded atmosphere. The handy on-site shop is well stocked and there is good access to and from the site. Enjoying a central location with marvellous views over idyllic countryside, Honeybridge Park makes for an ideal family holiday - children can play in perfect safety as the site is in a country lane with very little through traffic - or for anyone looking to get away from it all and enjoy some truly pastoral surroundings.

Honeybridge Park, Honeybridge Lane, Dial Post, West Sussex RH13 8NX Tel: 01403 710923

BILLINGSHURST
MAP 2 REF D4
6½ miles SW of Horsham on the A272

This attractive small town, strung out along Roman Stane Street, was, in the days before the railways, an important coaching town and several good former coaching inns, including the 16TH century Olde Six Bells, can still be found in the old part of the town. Although the Norman parish **Church of St Mary** was heavily restored by the Victorians it has, since 1884, featured a clock whose mechanism is a half size replica of Big Ben's.

ITCHINGFIELD
Map 2 ref E4

3 miles SW of Horsham off A264

The **parish church**, in this tiny village, has an amazing 600 year old belfry tower, the beams of which are entirely held together with oak pegs. During a restoration programme in the 1860s, workmen found a skull on one of the belfry beams and it is said to have been that of Sir Hector Maclean. A friend of the vicar of the time, Sir Hector was executed for his part in the Jacobite Rising of 1715 and, presumably, his old friend thought to keep his gruesome souvenir in a safe place. In the churchyard of this early 12th century building is **little priest's house** that was built in the 15th century as a resting place for the priest who rode from Sele Priory at Upper Beeding to pick up the parish collection.

BARNS GREEN
Map 2 ref E4

5 miles SW of Horsham off the A264

The Queens Head, just to the south of Itchingfield in Barns Green, is a marvellous country inn that is housed in two mid 18th century smuggler's cottages which still retain their cosy and quaint atmosphere. Bedecked with colourful hanging baskets and flower-filled tubs throughout the summer, the pub has an attractive patio area at the front and a secluded lawned beer garden to the rear. As unspoilt inside as the exterior, this delightful country inn is warm and invit-

**The Queens Head, Chapel Road, Barns Green,
West Sussex RH13 7PS Tel: 01403 730436**

ing. As with most buildings of this age, the ceilings are low but the interior is surprisingly large. Open fires add extra warmth in the winter which also show off the gleaming horses brasses that adorn the walls and beams. A friendly pub where all are welcome, host, Abigail Moore, has not only created the perfect place to enjoy a quiet drink from the bar's excellent range of real ales, but a mouthwatering menu of traditional pub food - with a special difference - is served throughout the week. A lively place that caters for everyone's needs, The Queens Head also hosts a variety of theme nights which include quizzes, bingo and murder mystery evenings.

RUDGWICK
MAP 2 REF D4
5½ miles NW of Horsham on the B2128

A typical Wealden village of charming tile-fronted cottages, the 13ᵀᴴ century village church has a fine Sussex marble font in which the shells of sea creatures have been fossilised into the stone.

The attractive **Mucky Duck** was originally built in the 1860s at the same time as the South Downs Link Railway was opened. Today, the railway is long gone and the track bed is now the pleasant South Downs Walk but the pub is still here serving an excellent selection of both food and drink. Hard to miss, the typical Sussex peg tiled exterior is bedecked with flower filled hanging baskets in the summer, the Mucky Duck is a warm and friendly place for all the family. Traditionally furnished and decorated, with a mass of exposed beams, open fires and a long copper topped bar that is said to be the longest in the county, visitors have a marvellous selection of real ales from which to choose. There is also a large collection of single malt Scotch whisky here as well as a range of Irish whiskies and more unusual spirits for the more adventurous. Since they came here in 1993, hosts Roger and Vera, along with their dog Woody and cat, Eric, have also put the Mucky Duck on the dining map of Sussex. With a

The Mucky Duck, Loxwood Road, Tismans Common, Rudgwick, West Sussex RH12 3BW Tel & Fax: 01403 822300

menu of traditional pub food, plus a mouthwatering range of lunchtime filled baguettes, a steak board, and their famous varieties of sausage, this is just the place for an interesting and relaxed evening out. Finally, Roger and Vera offer accommodation in a very well appointed guest room - there is a proposed extension to add a further six twin/double ensuite rooms one with access for the disabled. As well as welcoming children, the family pet is also made to feel at home here.

WARNHAM   MAP 2 REF E4
2 mile NW of Horsham off the A24

This small and well kept village is famous as being the birthplace of the poet Percy Bysshe Shelley. He was born, in 1792, at **Field Place**, a large country house just outside the village, and this is where he spent a happy childhood exploring the local countryside and playing with paper boats on the lake at the house. Famously, the young poet was cast out of the family home by his father who did not approve of his profession and while there are many Shelley memorials in the parish church Percy has no memorial. His ashes are buried in Rome, where he died in 1822, and his heart lies in his son's tomb in Bournemouth. The immaculate gardens of Field Place are occasionally open to the public.

HAYWARDS HEATH

On first appearances, Haywards Heath appears to be a modern town, situated on high heathland. However, the conservation area around **Muster Green** indicates where the old settlement was originally based. A pleasant open space surrounded by trees, which is believed to takes its name from the obligatory annual 17th century custom of mustering the militia, the green was the site of a battle during the Civil War. Here, too, can be found Haywards Heath's oldest building, the 16th century **Sergison Arms** which takes its name from the landed family who once owned nearby Cuckfield Park.

The modern town has grown up around the station to which Haywards Heath owes its prosperity as the two nearby villages of Lindfield and Cuckfield both refused to allow the railway to run through them when the line from London to the south coast was laid in the 19th century.

AROUND HAYWARDS HEATH

LINDFIELD   MAP 2 REF F4
1 mile NE of Haywards Heath on the B2028

This famous beauty spot is everyone's idea of the perfect English village: the wide common was once used for fairs and markets, the High Street leads up hill to the church and there are some splendid domestic buildings from tile hung cottages to elegant Georgian houses. The village is also home to **Old Place**, a small timber framed Elizabethan manor house that is said to have been Queen Elizabeth's country cottage and the cottage next door is said to have been Henry VII's hunting lodge. The 13TH century village church, as well as being on a hill top, also has an overly large spire and, in the days when the surrounding area was wooded, this was a useful landmark. Beside the churchyard is **Church House**, which was originally The Tiger Inn. During the celebrations after the defeat of the Spanish Armada in 1588, the inn supplied so much strong ale to the villagers that the bellringers broke their ropes and cracked one of the church bells. The inn, along with the village's other inns, were, during the 18TH and 19TH century busy coaching inns as Lindfield was an important staging post between London and Brighton.

ARDINGLY   MAP 2 REF F4
3½ miles N of Haywards Heath on the B2028

Chiefly famous for being the home of the showground for the South of England Agricultural Society, though there is some modern building, the old part of the village has remained fairly unspoilt. Here, too, is another of the public schools founded by the pioneering churchman Nathaniel Woodard in 1858. A large red brick building, with its own squat towered chapel, **Ardingly College** is set in glorious countryside. The village church, around which the old part of Ardingly is clustered, dates from medieval times though there is much Victorian restoration work. Inside can be found various brasses to the Tudor Culpeper family whilst, outside, the churchyard wall was used, in 1643, as a defensive position by the men of Ardingly against Cromwell's troops who came to take the Royalist rector.

To the west of the village, a tributary of the River Ouse has been dammed to form **Ardingly Reservoir**, a 200 acre lake which offers some excellent fishing as well as waterside walks and a nature trail.

Just north of Ardingly, at the top end of the reservoir, lies **Wakehurst Place**, the Tudor home of the Culpeper family which arrived here

Wakehurst Place

in the 15ᵀᴴ century. The present house, a striking Elizabethan mansion, was built in 1590 by Edward Culpeper and the house and estate was eventually left to the National Trust in 1963 by Sir Henry Price. Over the years, but particularly during the 20ᵀᴴ century, the owners of Wakehurst Place have built up a splendid collection of trees and shrubs in the natural dramatic landscapes of woodlands, valleys and lakes. Now leased to the Royal Botanic Gardens at Kew, the 500 acre gardens are open to the public throughout the year and, as well as the varied and magnificent display of plants, trees and shrubs, visitors can take in the exhibitions in the house on local geology, habitats and woodlands of the area. Wakehurst Place is also home to the **Millennium Seed Bank**.

Found on the outskirts of the village, **The Avins Bridge Restaurant and Rooms** is a delightful and distinctive red brick Victorian house that is well worth seeking out. Purchased in 1997 by the charming couple, Chris and Becky Barnard, they have transformed the former pub into a wonderful restaurant that provides guests with a splendid dining experience. Specialising in organic produce, the monthly changing à la carte menu provides a delicious selection of vegetar-

The Avins Bridge Restaurant and Rooms, College Road, Ardingly, West Sussex RH17 6SH Tel: 01444 892393 website: www.theavinsbridge.co.uk

ian, fish and meat dishes that are sure to tempt even the most jaded palate. Chris, who trained as a chef, uses both flair and imagination in putting together the interesting dishes and, to round off the meal, there is a mouthwatering list of puddings. (Special diets can easily be catered for with prior notice.) As the restaurant also has a full licence, both residents and non residents can enjoy a predinner drink in the attractive bar area, or on the patio if the weather is pleasant, and there is an extensive list of both new and old wines as well as English and organic wines. The four ensuite guest rooms and guest suite all match the same high standard met by the restaurant and, whilst maintaining the character and charm of the original house, they are also equipped with the latest technology including ISDN phone lines.

WORTH   MAP 2 REF F3
8 miles N of Haywards Heath off the B2036

For those with a particular interest in historic churches, the ancient settlement of Worth, which is now all but a suburb of Crawley, is well worth a visit. Considered by many to be one of England's best churches, the Saxon **Church of St Nicholas** was built between 950 and 1050 though, for some reason, it does not feature in the Domesday Book. Still in use today, the church is both massive and solid but the addition of a Victorian tower and broach spire masked its importance from a distance.

The Benedictine monastery and Roman Catholic boys' public school, **Worth Abbey**, lies to the east of Worth and it was originally built as the country house of a wealthy tycoon. Paddockhurst, as it was known, was built by Robert Whitehead, a 19TH century marine engineer who invented the torpedo but the house was greatly added to by the 1ST Lord Cowdray who purchased the property from Whitehead in 1894. Using Paddockhurst as his weekend retreat, Lord Cowdray, who had amassed a fortune through civil engineering works, spend thousands of pounds on improving the house, including adding painted ceilings and stained glass. After the lord's death, in 1932, the house was purchased by the monks as a dependent priory of Downside Abbey, Somerset and it became an independent house in 1957.

EAST GRINSTEAD   MAP 2 REF G3
10 miles N of Haywards Heath on the A22

Situated 400 feet above sea level on a sandstone hill, this rather suburban sounding town has a rich history that dates back to the early 13TH century when, in 1221, East Grinstead was granted its market charter. Throughout the Middle Ages, it was an important market town as well as being a centre of the Wealden iron industry. The name, Grinstead, means 'green steading' or 'clearing in woodland' and, though Ashdown Forest is a few miles away today, it was once a much more extensive woodland which provided much of the fuel for the town's prosperity.

Although there is much modern building here, the High Street consists largely of 16TH century half timbered buildings and this is where the splendid **Sackville College** can be seen, set back from the road. However, this is not an educational establishment as the name might suggest, but a set of almshouses that were founded in 1609 by the Earl of Dorset. The dwellings are constructed

Sackville College, East Grinstead

around an attractive quadrangle and they were built for the retired workers of the Sackville estates at Buckhurst and Knole. The parish **Church of St Swithin** stands on an ancient site but it only dates from the late 18th century as the previous church was declared unsafe after the tower collapsed in 1785. Built to the designs of James Wyatt, beside the porch are three graveslabs in memory of Anne Tree, John Forman and Thomas Dunngate, Protestants who were burnt at the stake in East Grinstead in 1665.

Before the Reform Act of 1832, only the occupants of East Grinstead's 48 original burgage plots (long, narrow housing allotments) were eligible to vote - making this one of the county's most rotten of boroughs. As was common practice elsewhere, the local landed family, the Sackvilles, would ensure that they acquired enough votes to guarantee a comfortable majority.

The arrival of the railways in 1855 ended a period of relative decline in the town and, today, East Grinstead is a flourishing place. Perhaps, however, the town will always be remembered for the pioneering work carried out at the Queen Victoria Hospital during World War II. Inspired by the surgeon, Sir Archibald McIndoe, great advances in plastic and reconstructive surgery were made here to help airmen who had suffered severe burns or facial injuries. Following McIndoe's death in 1960, the **McIndoe Burns Centre** was built to further the research and the hospital remains the centre of the Guinea Pig Club, set up for and by the early patients of the pioneering surgeon.

The **Town Museum**, housed in East Court, is a fine building that was originally constructed as a private residence in 1769. An interesting place which tells the story of the town and surrounding area, as well as the life of its inhabitants, the Greenwich Meridian passes through the town at this point giving visitors the opportunity to stand with one foot in the east and the other in the west.

To the south of East Grinstead lies **Standen**, a remarkable late Victorian country mansion that is a showpiece of the Arts and Crafts Movement. Completed in 1894 by Philip Webb, an associate of William Morris, for a prosperous London solicitor, the construction of the house was made using a variety of traditional local building materials and Morris designed the internal furnishings such as the carpets, wallpapers and textiles. Now fully restored, the house, which is owned by the National Trust, can be seen in all its 1920s splendour, with every detail correct right down to the original electric light fittings. Open to the public, the house is set within a beautiful hillside garden with views over the Ashdown Forest and the valley of the Upper Medway. From near Standen runs the **Bluebell Railway**, which offers a pleasant journey through the Sussex Weald to Sheffield Park, the railways headquarters, via the 1930s station at Horsted Keynes.

Also nearby lies another interesting house, **Saint Hill Manor**, one of the finest sandstone buildings in the county that was built in 1792 by Gibbs Crawfurd, the grandfather of the man who brought the railway to East Grinstead in the mid 19TH century. Other owners of the house include the Maharajah of Jaipur and Mrs Neville Laskey, a generous lady who accommodated the RAF patients of Sir Archibald McIndoe. The author, Ron Hubbard, was the house's last owner and it was he who oversaw the work to restore the manor to its former glory including the Monkey Mural that was painted in 1945 by Sir Winston Churchill's nephew, John Spencer Churchill.

Just a few minutes walk from the centre of East Grinstead, yet in a quiet, residential area, lies the **Town House**, an attractive red brick and timber style house that dates from the end of the 19TH century. The Town House has been managed by Elana since 1994 and she runs much sort after bed and breakfast accommodation which sees many guests returning time and time again. A warm and hospitable host, Elana likes to make all her guests feel at home and this is instrumental in the success of her business. As this is a large house there is plenty of room for the six guest rooms - three of which have ensuite showers - and there is also ample parking close by. Simply, but effectively furnished, this is a comfortable and well

Town House, 6 De La Warr Road,
East Grinstead, West Sussex RN19 3BN
Tel: 01342 324200/300310 Fax: 01342 315122

maintained house where all are able to relax and enjoy their stay. Breakfast is taken in the large and spotless modern kitchen, where guests prepare their own meal from the excellent variety of dishes laid out.

WEST HOATHLY
5½ miles N of Haywards Heath off the B2028

MAP 2 REF F4

Situated high on a ridge overlooking the Weir Wood Reservoir to the northeast, this historic old settlement grew up around an ancient crossing point of two routes across the Weald. The squat towered **village church** was begun before the Norman Conquest and, inside, there are a number of iron graveslabs of the Infield family from nearby Gravetye Manor. In the churchyard, on the south wall, is a small brass in memory of Anne Tree, one of the 16TH century East Grinstead martyrs. Lying in woodland just north of the village is **Gravetye Manor**, a splendid stone Elizabethan house that was built, in 1598, for the Infield family - a family of wealthy, local iron masters. Much later, in the 1884, William Robinson, the gardening correspondent of The Times, bought the house and, over the next 50 years, he created the splendid gardens which, in many cases, follow the natural contours of this narrow valley. Today, the manor is a first class country house hotel.

However, the village's most impressive building is undoubtedly the **Priest House**, a low half timbered 15TH century house that was built as the estate office for the monks of Lewes Priory who owned the manor here. This would originally have been one vast

Priests House

room but, in Elizabethan times, the building was altered to its present form. As recently as 1905, the building was all but a ruin. Now, however, the Priest House is a marvellous and typical cottage, filled with 18TH and 19TH century furniture, set in a classic English country garden. Now a museum belonging to the Sussex Archaeological Society, the charming furnished rooms contain many interesting articles from everyday village life and make for an informative and delightful visit.

BURGESS HILL

MAP 2 REF F5

3 miles SW of Haywards Heath on the B2113

This small town, which has recently undergone much central redevelopment, owes its existence to the arrival of the railway in the mid 19ᵀᴴ century. Though, compared to many of the settlements in the surrounding area, Burgess Hill is a relatively new addition to the landscape. It does, however, have a particularly spacious cricket pitch and some older buildings that remain from what was once a small settlement.

Originally from Cologne, Ingeborg Chadwick, who has lived in England since 1958, established **Kaffee Stube** in 1981 and with it she has brought a little of her native Germany to southern England. Found on the ground floor of an old cottage, this charming establishment has a friendly, intimate atmosphere that is enhanced by the wood burning stove, the old clock ticking on the wall and the gentle classical music playing in the background. The small but well chosen menu, naturally, specialises in German dishes and, as well as the mouthwatering gateaux, there are a number of tasty savoury meals from which to choose. As Ingeborg is also busy in the kitchen, customers can be sure of the authenticity

Kaffee Stube, German Coffee House, 155 London Road, Burgess Hill, West Sussex RH15 8LH Tel: 01444 236285

of the German goulash soup and the potato salad. Finally, over the coffee house is a comfortable self-contained guest room with bathroom that makes a pleasant base for a couple as well as for a family.

Surrounded by over seven acres of grounds which include a small wood and a duck pond, **The Homestead** is the attractive home of Sue and Mike Mundy. From their large family home, built in the late 1970s, this friendly couple offer superb bed and breakfast accommodation in a choice of four ensuite guest rooms (two of which are situated on the ground floor and have wheelchair access). As

The Homestead, Homestead Lane, Valebridge Road, Burgess Hill, West Sussex RH15 0RQ Tel: 01444 246899

with the rest of The Homestead, the guest bedrooms are both comfortably furnished and tastefully decorated and provide the visitor with real home from home hospitality. As well as serving a wide range of dishes for breakfast which includes fresh eggs and homemade preserves, the couple also welcome guests with tea and cakes taken outside in the glorious garden (weather permitting). Because The Homestead is found down a long private driveway, the situation is secluded and peaceful, and, to ensure a completely relaxing break for visitors, children under 12 years of age cannot be accommodated and there are kennels nearby for guests' dogs.

KEYMER
MAP 2 REF F5

5½ miles SW of Haywards Heath on the B2116

Situated between two tributaries of the River Adur, this old village was once a centre of smuggling - in 1777 over £5,000 worth of goods were seized by custom. Keymer is, however, better known for its famous works that are still producing handmade bricks and tiles. Surprisingly, though, the double spire of Keymer's Church of St Cosmas and St Damian (patron saints of physician and surgeons) is covered not with tiles but wooden shingles.

HURSTPIERPOINT
MAP 2 REF F5

5½ miles SW of Haywards Heath on the B2116

Surrounded by unspoilt countryside, this pretty village, which takes its name from the Saxon for wood - *hurst* - and Pierpoint after the local landowning family, was mentioned in the Domesday Book. The narrow High Street here is particularly attractive and, as well as the fine Georgian buildings, the tall village church was built to the designs of Sir Charles Barry, architect of the Houses of Parliament, in the 1840s. Another imposing building, dominating the country-side to the north of the village, is **Hurstpierpoint College** chapel. Like nearby Lancing and Ardingly, the school was founded in the 19TH century by Nathaniel Woodard.

To the south of the village lies the ancestral home of the Norman Pierpoint family. They settled here in the 11TH century close to their powerful relative William de Warenne and **Danny** was, in those days, a modest hunting lodge situated below the grassy mound of Woolstonbury Hill. In the mid 15TH century, the family had to flee after the then owner, Simon de Pierpoint, deliberately murdered some of his serfs and the house was burnt to the ground in retalia-tion. The site stood empty until, in the late 16TH century, Elizabeth I granted the estate to George Goring who built the impressive classic Elizabethan E shaped mansion seen today.

However, the history of Danny remains a somewhat turbulent story as Gor-ing, a staunch Royalist, was forced to give up his splendid mansion at the end of the Civil War. It was the Campion family, coming here in the early 18TH century, who added the Queen Anne south facing façade as well as remodelling the inte-rior by lowering the ceiling in the Great Hall and adding a grand, sweeping staircase.

Danny's finest hour came, in 1918, when the Prime Minister, Lloyd George rented the house and it was here that the terms of the armistice with Germany were drawn up to end World War I. A plaque in the Great Hall commemorates the meetings held here by Lloyd George's war cabinet and, during the time that the cabinet was here, Lloyd George was known to have walked up Woolstonbury Hill to seek peace and solitude. The house also saw service during World War II when it was occupied by British and Commonwealth troops. Today, Danny is privately owned but is occasionally open to the public.

CLAYTON

MAP 2 REF F5

6 miles SW of Haywards Heath on the A273

This small hamlet, which lay on a Roman road between Droydon and Portslade, is home to a rather ordinary Saxon church which has, inside, early medieval wall paintings. Though the date of the art work is unknown, they are undoubt-edly the work of artists from St Pancras Priory, Lewes, who were also responsible for many of the surrounding churche's wall paintings.

The settlement lies at one end of a mile long railway tunnel which was constructed in the 1840s to take the still busy London to Brighton track. An engineering wonder of its day, the northern end of **Clayton Tunnel** is domi-nated by a large Victorian folly, **Tunnel House**, that was built in a grand Tudor style to house the tunnel keeper.

On a hill overlooking Clayton stand two windmills, known rather unimaginatively as **Jack and Jill**. The larger of the pair, Jack, is tower mill dating from 1896, now without its sails, that fell into disuse in the 1920s and has been converted into an unusual private residence. Meanwhile, Jill a post mill that originally stood in Brighton, was brought here by oxen in 1852, has been fully restored and is still capable of grinding corn.

PYECOMBE
MAP 2 REF F5

7 miles SW of Haywards Heath on the A23

This ancient village stands on a prehistoric track that runs along the South Downs from Stonehenge to Canterbury. Home to one of the smallest downland churches, this simple, Norman building has a 12TH century lead font that survived the Civil War by being disguised by the parishioners in a layer of whitewash.

However, Pyecombe is renowned amongst farmers, and particularly shepherds, as being the home of the best possible shepherd's crook, the **Pyecombe Hook**. It was the crook's curled end, known as the guide, that made the Pyecombe Hook so special as it was a very efficient mechanism for catching sheep though it was hard to fashion. Throughout the 19TH and early 20TH centuries, the village forge turned out these world famous crooks and, though they are no longer made today, several rare examples can be seen in Worthing Museum.

POYNINGS
MAP 2 REF F5

8 miles SW of Haywards Heath off the A281

Once an iron working village, Poynings lies in a hollow below the steep slopes of **Dyke Hill** on top of which is situated an Iron Age hillfort. Just south of Poynings, and close to the hill, is one of the South Downs greatest natural features - the **Devil's Dyke**. A steep sided ravine, local legend has it that this great cleft was dug by the Devil who, one night, decided to drown the religious people of Sussex by digging a deep ditch out to the coast. Working in darkness he was half way to the sea when an old woman climbed to the top of a hill with a candle and a sieve. The light of the candle woke a nearby cockerel and his crowing alerted the Devil who, looking up, saw the candle light, through the sieve, and fled thinking that the sun was rising.

During Victorian times, the Devil's Dyke became a popular place from which to view the surrounding downlands and, as well as building a railway to connect the village with Brighton, a cable car was installed over the ravine. The cable car has now gone but the site is still a popular place with motorists, walkers and hang gliding enthusiasts.

FULKING
MAP 2 REF F5

9 miles SW of Haywards Heath off the A281

The layout of this pretty village, situated under the steep downland slopes, has changed little since the 16ᵀᴴ century when the population of sheep in the area far outweighed the number of people. Beside the aptly named ancient village inn, The Shepherd and Dog, there is a spring and stream which, today, is now channelled through a Victorian well house. For centuries, the spring and the stream, which then flowed along the road side, would be used for washing (or dipping) the sheep before the annual spring sheep shearing and shepherds would bring their flocks to Fulking in droves. After the task of washing the sheep, the shepherds would retire to the inn with their dogs for a well earned drink. The spring here provided the village with all their water until the 1950s when a mains water supply arrived.

SMALL DOLE   Mᴀᴘ 2 ʀᴇꜰ E5
10 miles SW of Haywards Heath on the A2037

Just to the north of this small downland village, is **Woods Mill**, the headquarters of the Sussex Trust for Nature Conservation. As well as a nature reserve and the nature trail around the woodland, marshes and streams, the site is also home to an 18ᵀᴴ century watermill which houses a countryside exhibition.

Surrounded by a secluded garden and grounds and with fabulous views over the Adur Valley as far as Chanctonbury Rings, **Golding Barn Restaurant** is a hidden place well worth seeking out. Dating back to the 12ᵀᴴ century this marvellous building was a sheep barn until the 1930s when it first became a much

Golding Barn Restaurant, Golding Barn, Henfield Road, Small Dole, West Sussex BN5 9XH Tel: 01903 879309 Fax: 01903 814248

sought after tea rooms frequented by several famous people of the day including Laurence Olivier. Following a fire in the 1970, when the thatched roof was destroyed, the damaged barn was reconstructed to restore it to as near its original condition as possible - minus the thatch. Today, it is a wonderful and well known restaurant run by Maggie Jones and Gilbert Bastyra. Specialising in modern British food, diners can enjoy the fruits of chef Rob Malyon's labours in splendid surroundings. The tables are set in traditional fashion with fine linen, china and glassware and the room itself is a delight, with exposed beams, flint stone walls and, through the windows, the glorious views. The everchanging menus, table d'hôte at lunchtime, à la carte in the evening and Sunday lunch, are a mouthwatering array of the finest fresh British foods, prepared with flair and imagination. Add to this the upstairs function room where there are art exhibitions periodically and this is a place not to be overlooked.

EDBURTON   MAP 2 REF E5
10 miles SW of Haywards Heath off the A2037

This tiny hamlet is named after Edburga, the grand daughter of King Alfred, who is said to have built a church here in the 10TH century. However, the present **Church of St Andrew** dates from the 13TH century and, inside, can be seen one of only three lead fonts remaining in the county. Though battered and dented from the days of the Civil War, when it was used as a horse trough, the font survived being melted down for ammunition. On top of the steep downland escarpment, which rises to its highest point here, stands **Castle Ring**, a mound and ditch which are the remains of an 11TH century fort.

HENFIELD   MAP 2 REF E5
8½ miles SW of Haywards Heath on the A281

Once an important staging post, the village not only has a couple of excellent old coaching inns but also some other fine buildings of architectural note. The church is Saxon and dates back to a charter of AD 770 though it was heavily restored in the Victorian age and only a few medieval features remain. However, the 16TH century cottage, known as the **Cat House**, is a pretty if rather eccentric building. Situated near the church, around the eaves can be seen a procession of wrought iron cats, with their paws outstretched as if chasing birds. This peculiar decoration is thought to have been put up by an owner whose canary was eaten by the vicar's cat.

CUCKFIELD   MAP 2 REF F4
1 mile W of Haywards Heath on the A272

Pronounced *Cookfield*, this small country town dates back to Saxon times and though it would be particularly charming if the name were to have been derived from the Saxon Cucufleda meaning 'a clearing full of cuckoos', it is more likely that it means 'land surrounded by a quickset hedge'. Situated on the side of a hill, during the 11TH century, Cuckfield belonged to the Norman, William de Warenne, who had a hunting lodge and chapel here.

Before the new turnpike road was built in 1807, Cuckfield stood on the main route from London to the south coast and, because of this, it became a busy staging post. George IV used to stop here on his way to Brighton and, in the 1780s, one particular stage coach was passing through here three times a day. A horse drawn coach service was maintained from here by an American right up until the beginning of World War I when the horses were needed for the war effort.

To the north lies **Borde Hill Gardens**, a splendid typically English garden of special botanical interest, that has been created in some 200 acres of spectacular Sussex parkland and woods. It was Colonel Stephenson Clarke who, by funding plant hunting expeditions to China, Burma, Tasmania and the Andes, established the splendid collection of plants and trees which, today, are still maintained by the Colonel's descendants. With carefully planted displays that offer a blaze of colour for most of the year and regular special events, this garden is well worth exploring.

HANDCROSS

MAP 2 REF F4

7 miles NW of Haywards Heath on the B2114

This little village, which stood on the old London to Brighton road, is home to two glorious gardens. To the southeast lie the superb National Trust owned gardens of **Nymans**. Though much of the house that stood on this estate was destroyed by fire in 1947, the empty shell provides a dramatic backdrop to one of the county's greatest gardens. At the heart of Nymans is the round walled garden that was created with the help of the late 19th century gardening revivalists William Robinson and Gertrude Jekyll. Elsewhere, the gardens are laid out in a series of "rooms", where visitors can walk from garden to garden taking in the old roses, the topiary, the laurel walk and the sunken garden.

Just northeast of Handcross is another smaller, though not less glorious garden, **High Beeches Gardens**. Here, in the enchanting woodlands and water gardens, is a collection of rare and exotic plants as well as native wild flowers in a natural meadow setting.

4 Brighton and the East Sussex Downs

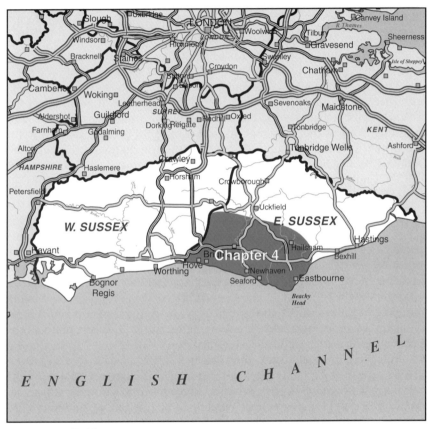

© MAPS IN MINUTES ™ (1998)

INTRODUCTION

This coastal area of East Sussex centres around the thriving resorts of Brighton and Eastbourne. Both began life as a quiet fishing villages but, following Royal visits, they developed rapidly at the beginning of the 19ᵗᴴ century. Brighton, the favoured holiday resort of the Prince Regent, is best known for the lavish Royal Pavilion, a splendid monument to exotic architecture and design. However, its Lanes, the narrow streets and alleyways of the old village are a real treat for antique lovers. Meanwhile, along the coast, Eastbourne, which shares many similarities has none of the grand architecture of its rival. Carefully planned and laid out by William Cavendish, the 7ᵀᴴ Duke of Devonshire, this is a genteel resort that is often combined with a visit to the spectacular chalk cliffs of Beachy Head.

The county town of Lewes dates back to Saxon times and it benefited greatly just after the Norman Conquest when both a great castle and the important St Pancras Priory were founded here by the Norman William de Warenne. Another coastal village also has links with the Norman invasion - Pevensey was the landing place of William, Duke of Normandy and his army.

Although many of the inland towns and villages have their roots in Saxon England they are also linked with artists and writers of the 19ᵀᴴ and 20ᵀᴴ centuries. Virginia Woolf and her husband Leonard lived at Monk's House, Rodmell, until Virginia's death in 1941 whilst her sister, Vanessa Bell, maintained her eccentric household at nearby Charleston Farmhouse, in Selmeston. The Elms at Rottingdean was the home of Rudyard Kipling until his success as a novelist forced him to move to a more secluded location in 1902 and the village of Ditchling became home to a group of artists and craftsmen and a centre for the Arts and Crafts Movement.

BRIGHTON

Before Dr Richard Russell of Lewes came here in the 1750s, this was an obscure little south coast fishing village called Brighthelmstone that dated back to medieval times. Dr Russell, a believer in the benefits of sea air and water who published a dissertation on *The Use of Sea Water in Diseases of the Glands*, set about publicising the village as a place to come to to derive relief from ailments and diseases by taking sea air, bathing and even drinking sea water. He also promoted the medicinal virtues of the mineral waters of St Ann's Well at Hove. By the time of the Prince Regent's first visit to the village, at 21 years of age in 1783, it was already becoming a popular place but still remained concentrated around the old village of Brighthelmstone. The effect of royal patronage on the village was extraordinary and the growth here was rapid. By the time of the Prince's last visit to Brighton, some 47 years after his first, the place had been completely transformed.

The Prince Regent, later to become George IV, was so taken with the resort that he first took a house here and, wishing a more permanent base, decided to build his famous **Royal Pavilion** in the resort. Initially a small farmhouse, that had been enlarged and added to over the years, in 1787 architect Henry Holland designed a neoclassical building with a dome and rotunda on the site. Finally, the pavilion seen today was created by John Nash, the architect responsible for London's Regent's Park and the Mall, between 1815 and 1822, in a magnificent Indian style. Based on a maharajah's palace, complete with minarets, onion shaped domes and pinnacles, the Royal Pavilion has been the most well known Brighton landmark for almost 200 years.

By contrast, the interior of the palace moves from the Indian subcontinent to the Far East and it is one of the most lavish examples of Regency chinoiserie in the world. The detail in the decoration is astonishing, with imitation bamboo everywhere and even the kitchens have not been left untouched for here can be found flamboyant cast iron palm trees.

Brighton Pavilion

The gardens surrounding this seaside pleasure palace are also the work of John Nash's elegant designs though one ancient oak tree here is said to be the one in which Charles II hid after the Battle of Worcester. However, though this is an unlikely claim the tree certainly predates Nash's splendidly laid out grounds. Beginning life as the Royal Pavilion's stables and once housing a riding school, **The Dome** - a dome shaped building dated 1805 - is now a superb concert hall. Meanwhile another part of this complex has been converted into the **Brighton Museum and Art Gallery**. Opened in 1873, this outstanding museum houses collections that are of both national and international importance. Among the marvellous displays are art nouveau and art deco furniture and decorative art, non western art and culture, archaeology from flint axes to silver coins and paintings by both British and European masters.

The creation of the Royal Pavilion and the almost permanent residence of the Prince Regent in the resort certainly sealed Brighton's fate as a much sought after seaside location and the town rapidly expanded - westwards until it met up with Hove and eastwards to **Kemp Town**, which was laid out by Thomas Reid Kemp, a local lord of the manor in the 1820s. Perhaps, the town's other great feature, after the pavilion, is the first example of town planning to take place here - the **Royal Crescent**. Built in the late 1790s, this is a discreet row of little houses which also proved a turning point as, from then on, all houses were built to face the sea rather than have their backs turned towards the coast.

For many visitors to Brighton a visit to **The Lanes**, the warren of narrow streets that represent what is left of the old village, is a must. Today, these tiny alleys are the preserve of smart boutiques and, particularly, antique shops, as well as some excellent restaurants, and despite the influx of both people and money, this is a wholly different place from the grandeur surrounding the Royal Pavilion and Crescent. Though even Brighton's **Town Hall** is Regency, there are some older buildings including the old **Parish Church**. Standing outside the old part of Brighton, ancient pictures show it as an isolated building that has long since been engulfed, the key feature within is the 12ᵀᴴ century drum shaped font. In the churchyard is a curious gravestone to Phoebe Hessel. Born in 1713, she served in the army as a private and, after her retirement, she came to Brighton where she died, aged 108, in 1821.

Another church that is worth visiting is the Roman Catholic **Church of St John** in Kemp Town. However, it is not for any ancient feature that visitors make their way here but to see the last resting place of Mrs Fitzherbert, who died in 1837. Maria Anne Fitzherbert, twice a widow, became secretly married to the future George IV in London in 1785 and they honeymooned in Brighton, where Mrs Fitzherbert also took a house that was said to be linked to the pavilion by an underground passage. Their marriage had to remain a secret as it was in fact illegal, being completely in breech of the Royal Marriages Act. Eventually, the Prince Regent, who could not acknowledge her publicly without renouncing the throne, broke off their affair in 1811.

Just a short distance way from the sea front lies **Preston Manor**, a delightful old house that is, today, restored and refurbished in the style of an Edwardian gentleman's residence. Beginning life as a 13ᵀᴴ century manor house, set within beautifully landscaped grounds, the manor was rebuilt in the 1730s and extended in 1905. Laid out on four floors, there are some 20 rooms to explore that range, literally, from the attics and nursery on the top floor to the servants' quarters at ground level. Within the pleasant grounds is a walled garden, a pets' cemetery and a croquet lawn.

Another lesser known place of interest in Brighton is **Stanmer Park and Rural Museum**. An excellent 200 acre country park centred around the fine early 18ᵀᴴ century mansion that was once the home of the Earls of Chichester. The park now also contains a large municipal nursery as well as glasshouses where flowers are grown. Meanwhile, behind Stanmer House is a unique collection of agricultural implements, including blacksmith's and wheelwright's tools. The late 17ᵀᴴ century well house that was designed to supply water to the house and was, originally, powered by oxen can be seen here too.

For those wishing to take a step back into their childhood the **Sussex Toy and Model Museum**, found under the arches of Brighton station, is the place. A fascinating display of trains, dolls, teddy bears, planes and much more will delight all members of the family - young and old. The world of natural history can also be discovered in Brighton, at the **Booth Museum of Natural History**. The creation of Edward Booth, a Victorian ornithologist, to his original collection of some 500 species of bird, assembled between 1865 and 1890, have been added displays of butterflies, fossils and animal skeletons. There is also a changing programme of temporary exhibitions and special events for both adults and children. Meanwhile, **The Sea Life Centre** concentrates very much on live creatures and it is home to the longest underwater tunnel in Europe. The tunnel winds through a series of underwater habitats where both fresh and sea water creatures can be viewed. However, though this is a an up to the minute centre it has not forgotten the Victorian architecture of the building in which it is housed and some of the original 19ᵀᴴ century display cases are still used here.

Like all self respecting seaside resorts in Britain, Brighton has a pier - **Palace Pier** - that is open every day of the year to amuse and entertain. For those looking for more refinement, there is the **Theatre Royal**, founded in 1774, that remains one of the country's best and loveliest provincial theatres.

Naturally, Brighton also has a whole wealth of places to stay, from small bed and breakfast establishments to splendid five star hotels, and, situated side by side on the front, are two superb hotels that symbolise Victorian holiday luxury. The white painted **Grand Hotel**, built in the 1860s, is maturing nicely whilst its neighbour, the **Metropole Hotel**, completed in 1890 has had a more chequered history. In 1984, during the Conservative Party Conference, an IRA bomb blew the hotel apart. Several people lost their lives in the tragedy and a great many more were injured. The hotel too suffered as the bomb had been strategically placed in its centre. However, just under two years later the hotel was once again fully open for business with no scars to show.

AROUND BRIGHTON

DITCHLING MAP 2 REF F5

6 miles N of Brighton on the B2116

This historic village (there are records going back to 765), which was known as 'Diccelingas' in Saxon times, was once part of a royal estate belonging to Alfred the Great before it was passed on to Edward the Confessor and then the Norman William de Warenne. The oldest building here, the parish Church of St Margaret of Antioch, dates from the 13ᵀᴴ century though detail from before the Norman Conquest can still be seen in the nave.

Close by the village green and opposite the church, stands **Wings Place**, an unusual Tudor house that is also known as **Anne of Cleves' House**. There is no record that the fourth wife of Henry VIII ever stayed here but she is thought to have acquired the property as part of her divorce settlement.

At the beginning of the 20ᵀᴴ century, this pretty village, at the foot of the South Downs, became the home of a lively group of artists and craftsmen including Eric Gill, Sir Frank Brangwyn and Edward Johnston. Today it remains a thriving place with many studios and galleries dedicated to the work of the artists and craftspeople who now live here.

To the north of the village lies **Ditchling Common Country Park**, a splendid nature reserve and beauty spot, with a lake, stream and natural trail. Meanwhile, south of Ditchling lies the 813 foot summit of **Ditchling Beacon**, the third highest point on the South Downs. Once the site of an Iron Age hill fort and almost certainly occupied by the Romans, the beacon was used as a vantage point from which fires were lit to warn of the coming of the Spanish Armada. A magnificent place from which to view much of this area - southerly over the coast and northwards over the Weald - the beacon was given to the National Trust in memory of the owner's son who was killed during the Battle of Britain in 1940.

Visitors wanting to discover more about the locality's long and interesting history should make a point of calling in at the superb **Ditchling Museum,** which is located in the Victorian former village school. From the Iron Age, there has been evidence of settlement in this area and the museum's Attree Room shows archaeological finds from prehistoric sites nearby and remains of Roman pottery dug up to the east of the village. Here is also the history of the parish church and more recently of 17ᵀᴴ century nonconformist worship in the village. As this remarkable village has an important place in the English Arts and Crafts movement, the museum features an important collection of work by 20ᵀᴴ century artists and craftsmen. Work can be seen by craftsmen including stonecarver and typographer Eric Gill, calligrapher Edward Johnston, painter and poet David Jones, weaver Ethel Mairet, silversmith Dunstan Pruden and artist Frank Brangwyn. The village school itself opened in 1838 and the schoolmaster's garden is stocked with fruits, flowers and vegetables as it would have been in the days of the first schoolmaster, George Verrall. Life of

Eric Gill Self Portrait 1927

Ditchling Museum, Church Lane, Ditchling, East Sussex BN6 8TB Tel & Fax: 01273 844744 e-mail: ditchling-museum.com

the village at home and on the farm is shown in the schoolmaster's cottage. Finally, as well as selling books on the craftsmen and local area, handmade ceramics and textiles, cards and traditional toys, the museum coffee shop serves tea, coffee, and homemade cakes.

PLUMPTON
Map 2 ref F5
6 miles NE of Brighton on the B2116

The village is divided in two: the modern Plumpton Green and the old village of Plumpton. **Plumpton Green,** to the north, grew up around the railway station and is the home of the famous National Hunt **Racecourse.** Spectators arriving by train should look out for the Victorian signal box which has been designated a listed building following the persistent efforts of local railway enthusiasts to preserve it.

Old Plumpton is centred around its flint built church which dates from the 12ᵀᴴ century. The elegant moated 18ᵀᴴ century **Plumpton Place** was substantially remodelled by Lutyens in the 1920s. The then owner, Edward Hudson, was a wealthy magazine proprietor who had already commissioned Lutyens to renovate his other country property, Lindisfarne Castle, off the Northumberland coast. A previous Tudor landowner, Leonard Mascall, was a great cultivator of apples - a tradition that is maintained at the East Sussex Agricultural College here in Plumpton.

The site of an early Bronze Age settlement can be found up a footpath opposite the college and, nearby, is a sandstone block which commemorates the Battle of Lewes, where Simon de Montfort defeated Henry III in 1264.

HAMSEY   MAP 2 REF G5

8 miles NE of Brighton off the A275

This must have once been an important place for, in 925, King Athelstan held a meeting of his counsellors at Hamsey Manor. Today, though, all that remains of this hamlet is the old church that is reached through the yard of a 400 year old farm.

BARCOMBE   MAP 2 REF G5

9 miles NE of Brighton off the A275

Situated on the banks of the River Ouse, which is tidal as far as this point, Barcombe is a tranquil place that was a particularly favourite picnic place with the Edwardians. As well as fishing and picnicking, artists would come here to paint the dilapidated mill buildings in this splendid Ouse Valley setting. An ancient settlement - there is evidence that the Romans were here - the village was described as having a church and three and a half mills in the Domesday Book. The half mill was one that spanned the river and the other half was accredited to the village of Isfield.

The parish church of St Mary once lay at the heart of the village but, as the Black Death came to the area, the village was decimated and those who survived rebuilt their houses a mile away to the north. There are marvellous views of the South Downs from the churchyard.

RINGMER   MAP 2 REF G5

9½ miles NE of Brighton on the B2192

This spacious village, familiar to anyone arriving at Glyndebourne by car, is one of the earliest recorded settlements in Sussex. Though nothing remains of the Saxon church that once stood close to the village's enormous green, there has been a place of worship here for over 1000 years. The present church was built in 1884 by William Martin - the man who is said to have made the first wooden wheeled cycle in Britain - after fires in the 16ᵀᴴ and 19ᵀᴴ centuries had burnt down the previous buildings. Inside the church can be found a very poignant memorial to the village's cricket team. During World War I they joined up en masse to fight at the front and, of the 34 club members who went to France, only six returned alive.

During the 17ᵀᴴ century, this rural village, in a roundabout manner, played an important part in the history of America. Two young women of the parish married men who went on to become influential figures in the birth of the United States: Guglielma Springett, the daughter of Sir William who supported Parliament during the English Civil War, went on to marry William Penn, the founder of the state of Pennsylvania; whilst Ann Sadler married John Harvard, the founder of Harvard University.

However, for all its history, Ringmer's most famous inhabitant was Timothy, a tortoise. He belonged to the aunt of the 18ᵀᴴ century naturalist Gilbert White, and, during his visits to see his aunt who lived here, White became fascinated by Timothy's activities. After his aunt's death, White continued to study the tortoise and, in *The Natural History of Selbourne* he describes the tortoise's lethargic movements. Timothy's carapace can be seen in the Natural History Museum, London.

LEWES
MAP 2 REF G5

7 miles NE of Brighton on the A27

The county town of East Sussex, Lewes is an historic settlement that occupies a strategically important point where the River Ouse is crossed by an ancient east to west land route. Much of the town's street plan dates from Saxon times when it was around 890, one of the Saxon capitals that was undoubtedly visited by Alfred the Great. It was also considered important enough to be allowed to mint currency. The Norman invasion in the 11ᵀᴴ century and William the Conqueror's success at Battle, however, really saw Lewes grow in stature.

Because of their closeness to the English Channel, William, when dividing up his new kingdom, gave the Sussex estates to his most trusted barons and the lands around Lewes were granted to his powerful friend, William de Warenne. It was de Warenne, along with his wife Gundrada, who began the construction of **Lewes Castle**, on two artificial mounds, and founded the great **Priory of St Pancras**. Today, a substantial part of the castle remains, including a section of the keep and two towers dating from the 13ᵀᴴ century. Though most of the buildings were pulled down and the stones used for other construction work, during the early 19ᵀᴴ century, the castle was owned by the Kemp family and they are responsible for the elegant Georgian façade to the **Barbican House** which covers the building's much older timbers. Overshadowed by the Barbican

Gate, the house is now home to the **Barbican House Museum** where relics found in the area, from prehistoric times through to the Middle Ages, are on display. Here too is the **Living History Museum**, with its superb scale model of Lewes set at the end of the 19TH century. There are also splendid views over the town available to anyone climbing to the roof of the keep.

Meanwhile, little remains of the Priory of St Pancras that, some suggest, William de Warenne founded not because he was pious but because of the brutal massacre of the Saxons he had witnessed at Battle. Built on the foundations of a small Saxon church, the priory and a great deal of land were given to the abbey of Cluny in Burgundy. At its height, the priory had a church as large as Chichester Cathedral, with outbuildings to the same scale, but all were destroyed at the time of the Dissolution in the 16TH century.

During the 14TH century a feud developed between the 4TH Earl de Warenne and Lord Pevensey. In order to settle their differences the two met, one May morning, under the walls of Lewes Castle. As they fought, Lord Pevensey cornered de Warenne and, as he was about to drive home his sword, Lady de Warenne began to pray to St Nicholas to save his life and she vowed that, should her husband be spared, her first born son would not marry until he had placed St Nicholas' belt on the tomb of the Blessed Virgin in Byzantium. At that moment, Lord Pevensey slipped and, as he fell, de Warenne drove home his sword. Years went by until the earl's eldest son, Lord Manfred, became engaged to Lady Edona and, halfway through a banquet to celebrate the 21ST anniversary of de Warenne's victory, a vision of the combat appeared to all the guests. Understanding at once that the vow must be fulfilled before their son's wedding, the earl and his wife sent Manfred to Byzantium. For over a year Lady Edona waited for him to return and, finally, his ship was sighted off Worthing. A welcoming party gathered and then, with every one watching, the ship struck a hidden rock and sank with all hands. Lady Edona, watching the ship go down, gave out a sigh and sank to the ground dead. Manfred's ship is said to be seen, each year, on the same day - May 17 - to flounder on the same hidden rock and a plinth stands in memory of Lady Edona who was buried where she fell.

Beside the priory ruins is a bronze memorial by the sculptor Enzo Plazzotti that was commissioned to commemorate the 700TH anniversary of the **Battle of Lewes**. Fought on Offham Hill, the Battle of Lewes took place in May 1264, between the armies of Henry III and Simon de Montfort. The night before the battle, de Montfort and his troops were said to have kept vigil in a nearby church whilst Henry III and his men had a wild and in some cases drunken evening at the castle. Whether this was the reason for the king's defeat or whether it was down to bad military tactics is open to debate.

Another monument in the town is the **Martyrs' Memorial** which was erected in 1901 in, rather belated, memory of the 17 Protestant martyrs who were burnt to death on Lewes High Street during the reign of Catholic Mary Tudor. The mainly Protestant inhabitants of Lewes found an outlet for their resentment at this treatment after the foiling of the Gunpowder Plot and, as a result, the **Bonfire Celebrations** which still take place here are elaborate affairs. Whilst the original reason for the enthusiasm has gone the celebrations take on a theme that stems from ancient Celtic pagan rites when fires were doused by water which represented the passing of the seasons from summer to winter.

Like Ditchling, Lewes has an **Anne of Cleves' House**, in this case an

Anne of Cleves' House, Lewes

early 16ᵀᴴ century Wealden hall house which, again, formed part of Henry VIII's divorce settlement with his fourth wife. Also like the house in Ditchling, it is unlikely that the queen ever set foot in the building. Today, the house is open to the public and the rooms are furnished to give visitors an idea of life in the 17ᵀᴴ and 18ᵀᴴ centuries.

As for the rest of the town, this is a place of parallel lanes and alleys that drop steeply down from the High Street. Here there are many interesting buildings that can be picked out including the house belonging to Dr Gideon Mantell, the 19ᵀᴴ century doctor and palaeontologist who discovered the first skeleton of an iguanodon, and **Shelleys Hotel** where Dr Johnson was a frequent visitor.

GLYNDEBOURNE   MAP 2 REF G5
9½ miles NE of Brighton off the B9192

Glyndebourne, a part Tudor, part Victorian country house, just a mile north Glynde village, is now the home of the world famous **Glyndebourne Opera House**. In the early 1930s, John Christie, a school master, music lover and inheritor of the house, married the accomplished opera singer Audrey Mildmay and, as regular visitors to European music festivals, they decided to bring opera to England and their friends. In the idyllic setting of their country estate, they built a modest theatre and, in 1934, Glyndebourne first opened with a performance of Mozart's *Marriage of Figaro*. However, their scheme was not an overnight success - on the second night only six people ventured here in evening dress - but the couple persevered and, by the outbreak of World War II, they had extended the theatre to accommodate 600. Since the early 1950s, Glyndebourne had gone from strength to strength and, as well as extending the theatre further, the repertoire has also increased. It was always Audrey's idea to begin with Mozart and not follow her husband's idea of starting with Wagner but the choice now ranges from the traditional to modern 20TH century works. Today, each summer season, from May to August, sees people venturing here dressed in evening gowns, laden with picnic hampers to enjoy a wide range of opera in a unique setting and eat their picnics in the grounds during the long interval.

GLYNDE
MAP 2 REF G5

9½ miles NE of Brighton off the A27

Situated at the foot of Mount Caburn, this small and attractive village is home to a splendid house and an ancient church. Overlooking the South Downs, **Glynde Place** was built in 1579 for William Morley, on the site of a medieval manor house, from flint and Normandy stone that was brought across the Channel in barges. An undistinguished family, the only member of note was Colonel Herbert Morley, a Parliamentarian who was also one of the judges at the trial of Charles I. Fortunately for the family, Morley did not sign the king's death warrant and so, at the Restoration, the family were able to gain his pardon from Charles II. Meanwhile, the house passed by marriage into the Trevor family and, in 1743, it was inherited by the Bishop of Durham. It was he, Richard

Glynde Place, Glynde

Trevor, who, with great foresight, left the exterior of the house untouched whilst turning the interior into classical 18TH century residence. The house is still in private hands and only open on a limited number of days during the year.

At the gates to the house stands the church that was built by the bishop in 1765 to the designs of Sir Thomas Robinson. Having recently visited Italy, Robinson was very enthusiastic about Renaissance architecture and, as a result, the church has a coved rococo ceiling, box pews and a gallery.

The village is also home of the black faced Southdown sheep that were first bred here by John Ellman which lived between 1753 and 1832. A benevolent farmer, he built a school for his labourers' children and, when they married, he gave the couple a pig and a cow. He even allowed the single labourers to lodge under his own roof. However, Ellman would not allow a licensed house in the village although he did not mind if his men brewed their own beer at home.

The distinctive **Mount Caburn**, to the west of Glynde, can be reached along a footpath from the village. Many thousands of years ago, this steep sided chalk outcrop was separated from the rest of the Downs by the action of the River Glynde. This process created a mound about 500 feet in height whose natural defensive properties have not gone unnoticed over the centuries. The earthwork defences of an Iron Age hillfort can still be made out near the summit and there is evidence of an earlier Stone Age settlement.

WEST FIRLE
Map 2 ref G6

10 miles E of Brighton off the A27

Though the village is known as West Firle, there is no East Firle - or any other Firle in the area. A feudal village of old flint cottages at the foot of the South Downs, it is dominated by **Firle Beacon** which lies to the southeast and rises to a height of 718 feet. As one of the highest points in the area, it was used by the Admiralty for a fire beacon to warn of the approaching Spanish Armada in the 16TH century but the importance of this vantage point has long been recognised. On the summit have been found, over the years, many relics including a Stone Age long barrow and a group of Bronze Age round barrows. There was also a Roman observation point here. Today, the summit can be reached by taking a small detour off the South Downs Way and there are some breathtaking views that make the climb well worth while.

Back in the village and set in its own idyllic parkland is **Firle Place**, the home of the Gage family for over 500 years. Built by Sir John Gage in the 15TH century, this marvellous Tudor manor house was greatly altered some 300 years later and today it will be familiar to many who have seen it as a backdrop for major feature films or as a location for television series. Still very much a family home, today owned by the 7TH Viscount, its rooms contain a wonderful collection of both European and English Old Masters as well as some rare and notable examples of French and English furniture and Sèvres porcelain. The magnificent deer park, which surrounds the house, was landscaped by Capability Brown in the 18TH century and it features a castellated tower and an ornamental lake.

RODMELL

MAP 2 REF G6

7 miles E of Brighton off the A26

This little village of thatched cottages is thought to have got its name from 'mill on the road' and, though no mill can be found here today, there is a Mill Road and, in the small 12ᵗʰ century church there is a reference to its old name 'Rodmill'.

However, the village's main claim to fame is that it was the home of Virginia and Leonard Woolf from 1919 until her death in 1941. The couple, escaping the confining intellectual world of the Bloomsbury set in which they were influential figures, settled at **Monk's House**, a delightful early 18ᵗʰ century farmhouse that is now in the hands of the National Trust and open briefly in the summer. Throughout their stay here, the couple, along with Duncan Grant and Vanessa Bell, filled the house with books and paintings and decorated it in a style similar to Charleston. The garden, which is lush with hollyhocks, dahlias and hydrangeas, gives good views over the downs across the River Ouse.

During her time here, Virginia wrote many of her best remembered works, but throughout her life she suffered great bouts of depression and mental illness. Finally, in 1941, she took her own life by wading into the river with her pockets full of stones. Surprisingly for the disappearance of such a well renowned figure, her body was not discovered for three weeks and then by some children playing on the riverbank. Her ashes, along with those of her husband who carried on living here until his death in 1969, are scattered in the garden.

SOUTHEASE

MAP 2 REF G6

7 miles E of Brighton off the A26

This tiny village, in a dip on the Lewes to Newhaven road, was first mentioned in a Saxon charter of 966, when King Edgar granted the church and manor here to Hyde Abbey in Winchester. Some 100 years later, at the time of the Domesday Survey, this was a flourishing village that was assessed as having 38,500 herrings as well as the usual farm produce. Inside the early **12ᵗʰ century church** is a copy of King Edgar's charter - the original is in the British Museum, London - and also an unusual organ that was built by Allen of Soho and installed in 1790. The only other organs of this kind that are believed to still be in existence are in Buckingham Palace and York Minster.

TELSCOMBE

MAP 2 REF G6

6 miles E of Brighton off the A26

Telscombe was once an important sheep rearing and a race horse training centre. In fact, the last man in England to be hanged for sheep stealing, in 1819, is believed to have come from the village. In 1902, the racing stables at Stud House trained the winner of the Grand National - Shannon Lass. The horse's owner, Ambrose Gorham, was so delighted with the win that he rebuilt the village church and each Christmas gave the children of the parish a book and a pair of Wellington boots.

PIDDINGHOE   MAP 2 REF G6
7½ miles E of Brighton off the A26

Set on a wide curve of the River Ouse, this village - whose name is pronounced 'Piddnoo' by its older inhabitants - was a great place for smugglers. Today, however, the ships and boats that tie up at the quayside below the church belong to deep sea anglers and weekend sailors. A picturesque place, with a host of 17TH century cottages and pleasant riverside walks, the golden fish weather vane on top of the church tower was referred to by Kipling as a dolphin but it is, in fact, a sea trout.

NEWHAVEN   MAP 2 REF G6
9 miles SE of Brighton on the A26

Newhaven itself is a relatively new settlement and it replaces the much older village of Meeching. Inhabited since the Iron Age, when a fort was built on Castle Hill, Meeching lay beside the River Ouse. However, in 1579 there was a great storm and the course of the river was diverted and its outlet to the sea moved from Seaford to near Meeching. Thus Newhaven was established at the new river mouth and it is now one of the county's two main harbours (the other is at Shoreham by Sea) with an important cross Channel ferry/hovercraft service and a cargo terminal.

Newhaven's rise began in the 19TH century and it grew steadily busier once the rail link with London was established in 1847. Two of the earliest visitors to use the passenger steamer service to Dieppe were the fleeing King and Queen of France, Louis Phillippe and Marie Amelie who stayed at the Bridge Inn in 1848 after their sea journey before continuing to London by train where they were met by Queen Victoria's coach and taken to Buckingham Palace. In order to maintain their anonymity, the couple registered at the inn under the rather original names of Mr and Mrs Smith.

Also in the 19TH century, during one of the periodic French invasion scares, **Newhaven Fort** was built. Consisting of a ring of casements constructed around a large parade ground, the fort was equipped with modern guns during World War II and also received several direct hits from German bombs. Today, it is a **Museum** where visitors can explore the underground tunnels and galleries and view the permanent Home Front exhibition. Meanwhile, the **Newhaven Local and Maritime Museum**, in Garden Paradise, contains a wealth of information relating to Newhaven's port, the town's history and its role in wartime. Here, also lies the **Planet Earth Exhibition**, which explores the world of natural history from millions of years ago to the present day.

PEACEHAVEN   MAP 2 REF G6
9 miles SE of Brighton on the A259

If nearby Newhaven is a recent town, Peacehaven must be considered just a fledgling village. The brainchild of wealthy businessman, Charles Neville, it was planned and designed during World War I and the intention was to call the new town Anzac on Sea in honour of the Australian and New Zealand troops who were stationed here before going off to fight in the trenches. However, after the Armistice, it was renamed Peacehaven which very much caught the mood of the time. Laid out in the grid pattern and with no immediate connection with either the South Downs or the coast, it remains a quiet place off the usual South Coast tourist itinerary.

Along the cliff top promenade there is a 20 foot tall monument to King George V that also marks the line of the Greenwich Meridian.

ROTTINGDEAN   MAP 2 REF G6
3½ miles SE of Brighton on the A259

Built in a gap in the cliffs between Newhaven and Brighton, Rottingdean was, naturally, a key place for smugglers at one time. However, more recently, it became the home of more artistic citizens. The artist Sir Edward Burne-Jones lived here for the last 20 years of his life in the rambling **North End House** by the green. During his time in Rottingdean, Burne-Jones designed seven windows for the originally Saxon parish church that were made up by William Morris. After his death in 1898, his wife, Lady Burne-Jones maintained her high profile in Rottingdean and, in 1900, caused uproar when she hung antiwar banners from her windows following the Relief of Mafeking.

Lady Burne-Jones was also Rudyard Kipling's aunt, and he lived here, at **The Elms**, for five years before moving to Bateman's in 1902. Overlooking the village pond, the gardens of The Elms are occasionally open to the public, Surrounded by old stone walls are formal rose gardens, wild and scented gardens and a wealth of rare plants.

Another famous resident of Rottingdean was J Reuter, a German bank clerk, who started a pigeon post to bring back news from abroad that expanded into the internationally respected world wide news agency.

WOODINGDEAN   MAP 2 REF F6
2½ miles E of Brighton on the B2123

A quiet residential area of Brighton which lies beyond the town's superb downland racecourse.

Built in the 1950s, the large, brick built **Toby Jug Inn** has retained its traditional unspoilt mid 20ᵀᴴ century feel despite several refurbishments over the years. A friendly and popular place, thanks to the hospitable hosts, Chris Garrett

**Toby Jug Inn, Cowley Drive, Woodingdean, near Brighton,
East Sussex BN2 6WD Tel: 01273 304100**

and Pam Otten, the pub is very much a local for those living in the surrounding area. As well as the spacious bar area, there is also a separate games room (complete with its own bar) where pool, snooker and darts can be played in pleasant surroundings. The range of real ales served here is supplemented by guest ales and those feeling hungry can take advantage of the traditional pub food that is served all day. However, that is not all the lively Toby Jug Inn has to offer as on Wednesdays there is a 'free mike' night where anyone can try their hand at entertaining the pub and, on Saturdays, there is always live music. As Chris is a former professional singer and guitarist, a high standard of band is ensured. Add to this the large garden and patio which offer wonderful views over the South Downs and this inn is certainly a place not to miss.

HOVE   MAP 2 REF F6

2 miles W of Brighton on the A259

Nestling at the foot of the downs and now joined to Brighton, Hove is a genteel resort that is famous for its Regency squares - such as Brunswick and Palmeira - and broad tree lined avenues. A former fishing village, as Brighton grew so did Hove with the major development taking place in the early 19ᵗʰ century when the seafront was built with its distinctive terraces. As well as the usual spoils of the seaside town, Hove is home to the Sussex County Cricket Club and hosts teams from all over the world at their ground.

The **Hove Museum and Art Gallery**, outside which stands the splendid wooden pavilion, **Jaipur Gateway**, an elegantly carved structure that was transported to England from Rajashtan in 1886, contains a whole host of exhibits on the history of the town. There is also a superb collection of 20ᵗʰ century paintings and drawings and 18ᵗʰ century furniture. For history of a different kind, the **British Engineerium**, housed in a restored 19TH century pumping station, has all manner of engines - from steam powered to electric. Many of the model and life size displays still work and the museum's working beam engine is powered up on a regular basis. Meanwhile, there is the Giant's Toolbox, a hands on display of gears and levers, cylinders and pistons that visitors can discover for themselves.

For one of the most spectacular views of the South Downs a visit to **Foredown Tower** is a must. Housed in a beautifully restored Edwardian water tower, there is a viewing gallery with Sussex's only operational camera obscura and a mass of computers and countryside data that tell the story of the local flora and fauna as well as the geography of the night sky.

Also in Hove, and rather out of place with the grand Regency squares and avenues, is **West Blatchington Windmill**. Built in the 1820s and still with all its original machinery working on all five floors, the mill has been restored and continues to grind flour. As well as watching the fascinating milling process, visitors can view an exhibition of agricultural equipment which includes an oat crusher and a threshing machine.

EASTBOURNE

This stylish and genteel seaside resort, which has managed to avoid both becoming too brash or disappearing into shy gentility, takes its name from the stream, or bourne, which has its course in the old reservoir in the area of open land that is now known as Motcombe Gardens. When George III sent his children here in the summer of 1780, it was, in fact, two villages, the larger of which lay a mile inland from the coast. Slowly the villages were developed and merged but it was William Cavendish, later the 7TH Duke of Devonshire, who really instigated Eastbourne's rapid growth as a resort from the 1850s onwards.

As much of the land belonged to the Cavendish family, the expansion was well thought out and managed agreeably which leaves, today, an elegant town, well known for its delightful gardens, that meets the demands that are laid upon it each summer. Among the first buildings that Cavendish had constructed are the handsome Regency style Burlington Hotel, St Saviour's Church, the town hall and the extremely elegant railway station. The classic pier was built in the 1880s and it remains one of the finest seaside piers in the country.

There are, however, several buildings which predate the intervention of William Cavendish. The original parish church, inland from the coast, dates from the 12TH century though it stands on the site of a previous Saxon place of worship. The excellent **Towner Art Gallery and Museum** is housed in a very sensible Georgian town house that was built by Dr Henry Lushington, a vicar of Eastbourne. It became home to the town's museum in the 1920s and, as well as the collection of 19TH and 20TH century British art, the history of Eastbourne is traced in the museum displays, from the time of the Romans through to the present day. Meanwhile, the development of the old village into a splendid seaside resort is told at the **Eastbourne Heritage Centre**.

As a coastal town, during the scare of French invasions at the beginning of the 19TH century, Eastbourne had its own defences. The **Martello Tower No 73**, one of 103 built along the south coast, is also referred to as the **Wish Tower**. Its rather odd name comes from the Saxon word 'wisc' which means marshy place and today the tower is home to a small **Puppet Museum**. Another Napoleonic defence, the **Redoubt Fortress**, was built between 1804 and 1810 on the seafront. Now the home of the **Military Museum of Sussex**, the exhibitions here cover some 300 years of conflict on land, sea and in the air and the highlights include, relics from the charge of the Light Brigade at Balaklava and Rommel's staff car from World War II.

The sea has always played an important part in the life of the town, from its early days as a fishing village and now as a resort offering a safe beach environment. Naturally, the lifeboats have played an important role through the years and, close to their lifeboat station, is the **RNLI Lifeboat Museum**. Here the history of the town's lifeboats, from 1853 onwards are charted through a series of interesting exhibits, including photographs of some of their most dramatic rescues.

Whilst the town is undoubtedly a charming and delightful place to explore and enjoy, perhaps finishing with an ice cream on the front listening to the military band playing under its famous bandstand, most people also wish to see **Beachy Head**. One of the most spectacular chalk precipices in England, with a sheer drop of over 500 feet in places, this very famous natural landmark lies just to the southwest of the town. The grand scale of the cliffs are brought home by the sight of the lighthouse, at the cliff base, which is completely dwarfed. Though Beachy Head is indeed a splendid and inspirational place it is also much favoured by those contemplating suicide - as a precaution the Samaritans have a special sign here.

Beachy Head Cliffs and Lighthouse

On the clifftop is the **Beachy Head Countryside Centre** which focuses on downland life, from the Bronze Age onwards, and includes numerous wildlife displays. This is also the end (or the beginning) of the **South Downs Way**, the long distance bridleway that was first established in 1972.

AROUND EASTBOURNE

POLEGATE
Map 2 ref H6

4 miles N of Eastbourne on the A27

The village grew up in the 19ᵀᴴ century around a railway junction and, today, it is almost a suburb of Eastbourne. Visitors coming here generally make for the **Polegate Windmill and Museum**, a splendid red brick tower mill, built in 1817, that is one of the few tower mills open to the public (though on a limited basis). Restored as early as 1867, all its internal machinery is in working order and here too is a small but fascinating museum of milling.

Though the village is relatively recent, the area has been inhabited for a long time and the remains of **Otham Priory**, founded in 1175, can still be seen and some of the buildings have been incorporated into a private house.

HAILSHAM
Map 2 ref H5

7 miles N of Eastbourne on the A295

This market town, which first received its charter in 1252 from Henry III, is a pleasant town where the modern shopping facilities sit comfortably with the chiefly Georgian High Street. Once a thriving centre of the rope and string industry, Hailsham had the dubious honour of supplying all the rope for public executions. Now, its rope and string are put to less lethal uses. Meanwhile, it maintains its rural roots and the three acre cattle market is one of the largest in Sussex - in the 19ᵀᴴ century shepherds from as far a field as Wales were known to bring their sheep here.

GOLDEN CROSS
Map 2 ref H5

8 miles NW of Eastbourne on the A22

Situated at Golden Cross on the A22 - between Uckfield and Hailsham - **Golden Cross Antiques** is a perfect stop for anyone interested in antiques and collectables. The large attractive building, dating from the 1800s, has, in the past been a grocers, drapers, post office and general store. Spacious, and with plenty of window space, this is an delightful spot to browse and linger. Visitors often refer to it as an Aladdin's Cave. With 30 years experience in the trade, the proprietor, Rhoda Buchan, has developed a wide knowledge of furniture and general antiques and has a particular interest in metalware. The dramatic array of copper and brass includes candlesticks, jardinieres, kettles, trivets, trays, oil lamps, coal helmets, fenders, fire iron, horse brasses, etc. Period and country furniture, small items of silver and pewter, and ceramics - mostly of English origin - make this a fascinating call for visitors from both home and abroad. Prices range from £3 to several hundred and there is truly something here for everyone. Open Monday to Saturday, 9.00 to 18.00 and

**Golden Cross Antiques, Fiveways House,
Golden Cross, near Hailsham,
East Sussex BN27 4AN Tel: 01825 872144**

most Sundays from 10.00 until 18.00 - or telephone for an appointment outside these hours.

PEVENSEY   Map 2 ref 16
4 miles NE of Eastbourne on the A259

Situated on the coast, in the shelter of Pevensey Bay, it was here, in 1066, that William the Conqueror landed with his troops prior to the Battle of Hastings. Then an important sea port, William left his half brother, Robert, here while he went off to defeat Harold. Many centuries earlier, Pevensey was the landing place for invading Roman legions and it was here they built a fortification to protect their anchorage. The fortress of Anderida, built around AD 280, was one of the first south coast defences and it was on this site, that Robert built a Norman fortress. The 11th century stone keep was joined, in the 13th century, by a stone curtain wall and, unlike many medieval castles, **Pevensey Castle** seemed well able to withstand attack. Following the Battle of Lewes, Simon de Montfort lay siege here and again Pevensey Castle withstood. However, the structure gradually fell into disrepair but it was brought back into service, briefly, during the advance of the Spanish Armada and again during World War II. Today, the castle is besieged by visitors who can not only explore the ruins but also follow its history, from the days of the Romans to the mid 20th century.

In the rest of the village there are an unusually high number of fine medieval buildings including the **Mint House**, a 14th century building that lies outside the castle gates. Coins have been minted on this site since 1076 and, though it is now an antiques showroom, visitors can see the priest's secret room and King Edward VI's bedroom. Any self respecting old building has a ghost and the Mint House is no exception. In the 1580s an Elizabethan woman, the mistress of the London merchant Thomas Dight, lived at the house and, on coming back unexpectedly, Dight found her in bed with her lover. Incensed with jealousy, Dight ordered his servants to cut out her tongue and hold her whilst she was made to watch her lover being roasted to death over a fire. The lover's body was thrown into the harbour and the mistress lead to an upstairs room where she starved to death. Another resident of the Mint House was Andrew Borde, the court physician to Henry VIII and also his unofficial jester. An interesting man, Borde was born in 1490, took orders, studied medicine in Europe and acted as a spy for Thomas Cromwell. A recognised wit of his day, his humour lead to his downfall and he died in prison after being tried on a trumped up charge by a gentleman he had satirized.

In the days prior to the founding of the Royal Navy, Pevensey served as one of the nation's Cinque Ports - that is to say, it was granted certain privileges by the Crown in return for providing ships and men in defence of the south coast.

Inland, lies the area of drained marshland known as the **Pevensey Levels**. At one time this was an area of tidal mudflats which were covered in shallow salt pans: since then it has been reclaimed for agricultural use and is now covered in fertile arable fields.

Situated within sight of Pevensey Castle, **Castle View Caravan Park and Camping Site** is a well established park that is also extremely well placed for the attractions of the surrounding area. Covering some 15 acres, this spacious site has plenty of room for the static and touring caravans and campers that find this the perfect place for a family holiday base. Open from March to November, the facilities found here include electric hook-ups, bathrooms as well as showers in the toilet block, and a gas exchange service. However, what draws holiday makers to Castle View are the well maintained pitches, the welcome

Castle View Caravan Park and Camping Site, Eastbourne Road, Pevensey Bay, East Sussex BN24 6DT Tel: 01323 763038

offered to everyone, including children and dogs, and the relaxing and peaceful atmosphere. Fortunately, those who do not have a tent or a caravan can still enjoy the delights found here as there are a number of static caravans for hire throughout the season.

WESTHAM

MAP 2 REF H6

4 miles NE of Eastbourne on the B2191

This pretty village is home to one of the most ruggedly beautiful churches in Sussex. Dating from the 14TH century and much patched and braced over the years, inside the parish church there is a memorial to John Thatcher who died in 1649 and left his estate to the 'Old Brethren' in the hope that, one day, Roman Catholicism would, once again, be the religion of England.

Just a couple of miles from the south coast and surrounded by grazing land, **Fairfields Farm Caravan and Camping Park** is a well maintained family run site that has been open for over 20 years. Exclusively for the use of touring caravans and campers, this attractive grassland site provides holiday makers with all the modern comforts including electric hook-ups, hot running water in the shower block, and a laundry room. Covering some four acres, the 60 camping and caravan pitches are well spaced and mature trees and hedges provide further privacy. As well as running the campsite, the family also own and man-

Fairfields Farm Caravan and Camping Park, Eastbourne Road, Westham, Pevensey, East Sussex BN24 5NG Tel: 01323 763165 Fax: 01323 469175 e-mail: fairfields.farm@btinternet.com website: www.btinternet.com/~fairfields.farm

age the surrounding farmland which is given over to sheep and cattle. From the site is a picturesque walk that takes in much of this meadowland and the farm's duckpond, peacock house, and chicken enclosure. Children will also enjoy meeting the farm's ponies and donkeys, including Ginny, the Shetland pony. Finally, Fairfields Farm has a well stocked fishing lake, where campsite residents can fish for roach, rudd, perch, and tench.

EAST DEAN

MAP 2 REF H6

3 miles W of Eastbourne off the A259

This charming village at the foot of the South Downs is one of the county's most picturesque, with its village green surrounded by a pub, flint cottages and an ancient church. Once a favourite haunt of smugglers, they used to meet at the **Tiger Inn**, a splendid 13ᵀᴴ century inn that for several centuries used this name before anyone realised that the animal on the local Bardolf family's coat of arms was not a tiger but, in fact, a leopard.

During the 18ᵀᴴ century, the local parson, Jonathan Darby, is said to have made a cave in the nearby cliffs from which he could display a huge lantern on stormy nights to warn sailors of the hidden rocks. However, some say that the reason for his retreat to the caves was actually to get away from Mrs Darby.

Just south of the village, right on the coast, is **Birling Gap**, a huge cleft in the cliffs which offers the only access to the beach between Eastbourne and Cuckmere Haven. Naturally, this was a great place for smugglers who landed their contraband here before making their way up the steep steps to the cliff top. This stretch of the coast, during the 18ᵀᴴ century, was managed by a particularly notorious gang led by Stanton Collins. He had his headquarters in Alfriston and, on one particular night, the gang are said to have moved the lumps of chalk from the cliff path so that pursuing customs officers could not find their way. One unfortunate officer fell over the cliff edge but miraculously held on by his finger tips. Collins' gang came upon him and, after listening to his pleas to rescue him, they stamped on his fingers and he fell to his death.

To the east of the gap lie the **Seven Sisters**, huge great blocks of chalk, the highest is 260 feet, which guard the coast between Eastbourne and Seaford.

FRISTON

MAP 2 REF H6

3½ miles W of Eastbourne on the A259

This is rather more a hamlet than a village, as only a part Norman church and a Tudor manor house can now be found around the village pond. The **churchyard**, however, is interesting as it contains the grave of the composer Frank Bridge, one of the pioneers of 20ᵀᴴ century English music and also the teacher of Benjamin Britten. Born in Brighton, Bridge lived in Friston for much of his life though he died in Eastbourne in 1941 - the south door was placed here in his memory. The village pond, too, has a claim to fame as it was the first in the country to be designated an ancient monument.

To the north and west of the village lies **Friston Forest**, 1600 acres of woodland that were planted in 1927 by the Forestry Commission. Among the fast growing pine trees slower growing broad leaved trees have been planted in this ancient beech forest that will eventually mature. There is a waymarked circular tour through the forest.

WEST DEAN

Map 2 ref H6

5 miles W of Eastbourne off the A259

Though the village is only a couple of miles from the south coast and close to Eastbourne, its position, hidden among trees in a downland combe, gives an impression that it is an isolated, timeless place. King Alfred is thought to have had a palace here and no more idyllic spot could be found for such a place. Known as Dene in Saxon times, Alfred the Great is also said to have kept a great fleet here on the River Cuckmere, which, then, formed a much deeper and wider estuary.

The village is now the home of **Charleston Manor**, an ancient house that was originally built in 1080 for William the Conqueror's cupbearer. Recorded in the Domesday Book as Cerlestone, the house has been added to over the years and it forms the centrepiece of a remarkable garden. Planted in the narrow valley, just north of Westdean's centre, the garden has more the feel of a Continental rather than an English garden with its parterres and terraces.

SEAFORD

Map 2 ref G6

8 miles W of Eastbourne on the A259

Once a thriving port on the River Ouse, Seaford was also a member of the confederation of Cinque Ports. Following the great storm in the 16TH century which changed the course of the River Ouse, Seaford lost its harbour and also its livelihood to the newly established Newhaven. Traces of the old medieval seafaring town can still be seen around the old church but, overshadowed by Brighton and Eastbourne on either side, the town never gained the status of its neighbours. The building of the esplanade in the 1870s did

Seaford Head Nature Reserve

bring some development as a modest resort but the constant pounding of the sea, particularly in winter, have kept the development small.

However, during the threat of a possible French invasion in the early 19TH century, Seaford was considered important enough to be the site of the most westerly Martello Tower - this one number 74. Today it is the home of the **Seaford Museum of Local History** and amongst the exhibits in this friendly and lively museum are a World War II kitchen, radio sets, vintage lavatories and mementoes from shipwrecks. From the roof of the tower there are magnificent views over the town and beyond as well as the tower's original cannon.

To the west of the town lies **Seaford Head**, an excellent place from which to view the Seven Sisters. The nature reserve here is home to over 250 species of plants and the reserve supports a wealth of wildfowl on its 308 acres of mudflats, meadowland and downland.

LITLINGTON

MAP 2 REF H6

6 miles NW of Eastbourne off the A259

Dating back to Saxon times, this village lies on the River Cuckmere at a point where the valley is narrowed by two downland spurs. This unspoilt village, however, is best known for the **Litlington Tea House** which first opened over 100 years ago. Since then little has changed and visitors can still enjoy a full homemade afternoon tea in its relaxed and old fashioned atmosphere. The only true difference is the style of dress and the cars in which the customers arrive. The gardens around the tea house are equally idyllic and, sheltered from the road by ancient trees, during the summer the teas are served on the grassy terrace.

JEVINGTON

MAP 2 REF H6

3½ mile NW of Eastbourne off the A22

This old smugglers' village was established during the time of Alfred the Great by another Saxon called Jeva. Inside the parish church, which can be found up a tree lined lane, there is a primitive Saxon sculpture and the tower dates from the 10TH century. During the 18TH century, when smuggling was rife in the area, the local gang brought their illegal goods up here from Birling Gap and stored them in the cellars of the village rectory. The gang's headquarters were the local inn and, conveniently, their leader was the innkeeper who was also the ringleader of a group of highwaymen until he was hanged in the 1760s.

ALFRISTON

MAP 2 REF H6

6 miles NW of Eastbourne off the A27

Alfriston is one of the oldest and best preserved (and, consequently, most popular) villages in Sussex and it is also convenient for the major holiday resorts. The settlement was founded in Saxon times and it grew to become an important port on the River Cuckmere and a market town. The old market cross still stands in the square and it is only one of two left in the county (the other is in Chichester). However, this has not escaped the ravages of time as it was smashed by a lorry and repaired by replacing the shaft.

One of the oldest buildings remaining in the town is the **Star Inn**, that was built in the early 15TH century as a resting place for pilgrims on their way to and from the shrine of St Richard at Chichester. Inside can still be seen the original medieval carvings of animals on the ceiling beams. Another ancient inn, the **Market Cross**, had no less than six staircases and, during the 19ᵀᴴ century was the headquarters of the notorious gang of smugglers led by Stanton Collins. Though he was never arrested for smuggling, Collins was eventually caught for sheep stealing and, as punishment, was transported to Australia. It was tales of Collins and other local gangs which inspired Rudyard Kipling, living at nearby Rottingdean, to write his atmospheric poem, *A Smuggler's Song*.

The former prosperity of this town is reflected in its splendid 14ᵀᴴ century parish church that is often referred to as 'the Cathedral of the Downs'. As recently as the 1930s, local shepherds would be buried here with a scrap of raw wool in their hand - a custom which served to inform the keeper of the gates of heaven that the deceased's poor church attendance was due to his obligation to his flock.

Beside the church is the thatched and timbered **Clergy House**, the first building to be acquired -for £10 - by the National Trust, in 1896. A marvellous example of a 14ᵀᴴ century Wealden hall house, its splendid condition today is due to the skilful renovation of Alfred Powell who managed to save both its crown pot roof and the original timbers. Visitors to the house, which has limited opening, can see an interesting exhibition inside on medieval construction techniques. The house is surrounded by a magnificent and traditional cottage garden that includes rare flowers that have been grown since Roman times but are almost lost to cultivation.

By contrast, to the north of the village lies **Drusillas Park**, a child friendly zoo that promises to be a hit with all the family. As well as housing over 90 species in imaginative and naturalistic enclosures there is also a creative play area, a train ride and attractive gardens.

WILMINGTON

Map 2 ref H6

5 miles NW of Eastbourne off the A27

This delightful village, with its mix of building styles, is home to the historic remains of **Wilmington Priory**. Founded in the 11ᵀᴴ century by William the Conqueror's half brother, Robert de Mortain, as an outpost of the Benedictine Abbey of Grestain in Normandy, the priory was well into decline by the time of the Dissolution. Many of the buildings were incorporated into a farmhouse, but other parts remain on their own including the prior's chapel which is now the parish church of St Mary and St Peter.

However, the dominant feature in Wilmington is its famous **Long Man**, that is cut into the chalk of Windover Hill and took its present form in 1874. There is much debate about the age of the Long Man and archaeologist and historians have been baffled for centuries. The earliest record of this giant is dated 1710 but this is inconclusive as it could be prehistoric or the work of an artistic monk from the local priory. However, what is known is that, at over 235 feet high, it is the largest such representation of a man in Europe. The giant, standing with a 250 foot long shaft in each hand, is, in many ways remarkable as, the design takes account of the slope of the hill and appears perfectly proportioned even when viewed from below. Covered up during World War II as the white chalk was thought to be a navigation aid to German bombers, it was outlined in concrete blocks in 1969.

Just a quarter of a mile from The Long Man lies the **Wishing Well Tea Rooms and Bed and Breakfast**, a family run establishment owned by Teresa Farrier. With the help of her mother, Ros, Teresa provides excellent home from home accommodation in a choice of two rooms in her charming home. Over 250 years old, this attractive typical Sussex house, is very aptly named as there is an old wishing well in the garden. In the Wishing Well's front garden are the tea rooms, where afternoon tea has been served since Victorian times. Built in same style as the house, the tea rooms, with the small patio

Wishing Well Tea Rooms and Bed and Breakfast, Wilmington, Polegate, East Sussex BN26 5SG Tel: 01323 487967

to the front, is the ideal place for all manner of light meals, set teas and homemade cakes, as well as a refreshing pot of tea. Here, too, customers can view and purchase all manner of craft items, many of which are locally made, to remind them of their visit.

ALCISTON
MAP 2 REF G6
7½ miles NW of Eastbourne off the A27

This quiet hamlet, which once belonged to Battle Abbey, became known as the "forgotten village" after its inhabitants left following the ravages of the Black Death and settled close by. The villagers left, amongst other buildings, a 13TH century church, which had been built on a hill on the foundations of a Saxon structure to avoid flooding, and 14TH century Alciston Court, that was once used by the monks. During the Middle Ages, the tenant farmers paid a rent to the abbot of Battle in the form of one tenth of their annual farm output and, at harvest time each year, this was brought to the abbey's vast medieval tithe barn which can still be seen looming in front of the church. After the village was abandoned, Alciston Court became a farmhouse. The remains of a large **medieval dovecote** can also be seen close by. During the winter, large numbers of pigeons would be kept here to supplement the villagers' dreary winter diet.

SELMESTON   MAP 2 REF H6
8 miles NW of Eastbourne off the A27

This ancient hamlet, which is sometimes misleadingly pronounced 'Simson', was the site where, during the 1930s, archaeologists discovered tools, weapons and pottery fragments in the churchyard which are thought to date from the New Stone Age. However, though the finds are interesting in themselves, Selmeston is better remembered as being the home of Vanessa Bell and her interesting domestic arrangements. Her house, **Charleston Farmhouse**, lies just west of the village and it was discovered by Vanessa's sister and her husband, Virginia and Leonard Woolf, when she was looking for a country retreat for herself. Vanessa, an artist, moved here in 1916 with her art critic husband, Clive, and her lover, fellow artist Duncan Grant.

From then on and over the next 50 years, the house played host to the intellectual and artist group that became known as the Bloomsbury set and, for a time, both David Barnett and Maynard Keynes also joined the household. Other frequent visitors included Virginia and Leonard Woolf, who lived not far away at Rodmell, EM Forster and Roger Fry. During the 1930s, the interior of the house was completely transformed as the group used their artistic skills to cover almost every wall, floor, ceiling and even the furniture with their own murals, fabrics, carpet and wallpapers. They hung their own paintings on the walls, including a self portrait of Vanessa Bell and one of Grace Higgens, the valued housekeeper. The garden of the house too was not forgotten and a delightful walled cottage garden was created at the same time with carefully laid out mosaic pathways, tiled pools, sculptures and a scented rose garden. Following Duncan Grant's death in 1978, a trust was formed to save the house and garden, restoring them to their former glory. This unique task has been described as 'one of the most difficult and imaginative feats of restoration' to be carried out in Britain. The property is open to the public on a limited basis.

An unexpected treat at Selmeston is **Silletts Cottage Restaurant**, a Grade II listed Sussex farmhouse, with part of the building dating back to 1540 when it was first built and named 'Church Farm' because its land was adjacent to the church. The date of the building is known, as it has been found carved on an exposed beam in the loft. The original building consisted simply of two downstairs front rooms, which are now a marvellous restaurant offering all the ingredients for a perfect meal in this lovely country setting. It is open for lunch and dinner seven days a week. Here can be had wonderful homecooked meals

**Silletts Cottage Restaurant, Selmeston, near Polegate,
East Sussex BN26 6TZ Tel: 01323 811343 Fax: 01323 811743
e-mail: ronsillett@compuserve.com
website: www.sillettscottagerestaurant.co.uk**

with a fine bottle of wine in a quiet, charming, relaxed atmosphere, which would be as pleasurable in summer as winter. In the summer guests can feast their eyes on views of the Downs, and in the winter they can relax in front of the crackling log fire in the cocktail lounge.

Ron Sillett's chefs, Neil Wakefield and Steve Anderson, prepare all of the dishes. They are always looking for new recipes, so if any visitor has one tucked away in a kitchen drawer do bring it along and show Ron. Silletts Cottage is quite small, and only accommodates a maximum of 40 customers. Lunch is from a snack to a full à la carte with no minimum charge. Dinner is a fixed price with no hidden extra costs. Personal service is terribly important to Ron and his staff. They look after their guests superbly and genuinely want to know if there is anything they can do to please them further. Customers are sure to enjoy every minute of their visit here and will no doubt join the ranks of those who return again and again.

RIPE   MAP 2 REF H5
9 miles NW of Eastbourne off the A27

Lying at the corner of a road grid laid out by the Romans, this quiet little village, obviously, has a long history. An attractive community, where there can be found a cottage faced with a remarkable set of wood carvings, Ripe lies on the fertile plain below the South Downs.

Originally built as farmworkers' cottages and once part of the Village Hall, **The Lamb Inn** is a charming old pub that dates from the late 18TH century. Very much an English country inn, The Lamb has been managed by Graham and Samantha since 1997, with the help of their three friendly dogs, and it is a place well recognised for its warm and friendly atmosphere and excellent food and drink. The interior is very traditional and stepping inside is just like walking back in time. Wood abounds, in the ceilings and in the wall panelling and, to

The Lamb Inn, Church Lane, Ripe, Near Lewes, East Sussex BN8 6AS
Tel: 01323 811280 e-mail: graham@the-lamb.co.uk

add further warmth, there are several open fires. The bar and restaurant areas comprise small alcoves and rooms which make for a cosy and intimate atmosphere. As well as being well known for the high standard of the selection of real ales on tap behind the bar, there is also an excellent wine list and all the usual beers and lagers from which to choose. Food too is a popular attraction of The Lamb and Anita Lucioni is responsible for the majority of the interesting and mouthwatering dishes that make up the tempting menu. Using fresh produce from local suppliers where possible, this is an excellent place to find, whether for lunch or dinner.

UPPER DICKER
8 miles NW of Eastbourne off the A22

MAP 2 REF H5

This hamlet, which overlooks the River Cuckmere, is centred around a minor crossroads in an area that was once known as 'Dyker Waste'. In 1229, Augustinian canons chose this as the site for the beautiful **Michelham Priory**. Founded by Gilbert de Aquila, the Norman Lord of Pevensey, the six acre site is surrounded on three sides by the River Cuckmere and on the other by a slow flowing moat - England's longest water filled medieval moat. The slow moving water is still used to power an old mill where traditionally ground flour is produced in small batches. A splendid gatehouse to the priory was added in the 14ᵀᴴ century and the priory continued to flourish until it was dissolved by Henry VIII in 1587.

After the Dissolution the priory came into the hands of first the Pelham family and then the Sackville family who, in the 300 years of their ownership, incorporated some of the priory's buildings into a Tudor farmhouse which went on to become the focal point of a large agricultural estate. Today, the grand Tudor farmhouse rooms are furnished with a collection of Dutch paintings, Flemish tapestries and old English furniture and the gatehouse is home to a group of brass rubbings and a reconstructed forge.

Michelham Priory

Michelham Priory Gardens are equally interesting and they cover a range of styles. To the south of the house is a physic herb garden containing plants that were, and still are, grown for their medicinal and culinary benefits. There is also a recreated cloister garden which illustrates the ability of the original monks to combine a pleasing garden with one that requires little maintenance. An Elizabethan barn can also be found in the grounds of the priory as can the working watermill, whilst, the river and moat attract a variety of waterfowl throughout the year.

LAUGHTON Map 2 ref G5
11 miles NW of Eastbourne on the B2124

This scattered village, isolated on the Glynde Levels, was once home to flourishing marble mines, potteries and a brickworks. In fact, Laughton Place, built in 1534, was one of the first brick buildings constructed in Sussex. The interior of the village church, which lies some way from the village centre, is dominated by a stone war memorial which features a soldier and sailor who have been carved in minute detail.

Set in beautiful countryside with splendid views over the South Downs, **Stone Cross Farm** is a traditional Sussex peg tiled farmhouse dating from the 17ᵀᴴ century. Now the home of Julia and John Fenton, along with their three children, this friendly couple have been offering relaxed and comfortable bed and breakfast accommodation since 1996. There are two spacious guest rooms, which can each easily take a family, and which have both been tastefully decorated and furnished without loosing the house's original features. The same is true of the other ground floor public rooms which comprise a comfortable lounge over-

**Stone Cross Farm, Laughton, Lewes, East Sussex BN8 6BN
Tel & Fax: 01323 811500**

looking the charming walled garden and the dining room with its exposed beams and large inglenook fireplace. A lovely place for children, not only can guests enjoy the gardens but the surrounding fields make a superb natural playground. As well as the homecooked breakfast served each morning, evening meals are also available by arrangement.

HALLAND   Map 2 ref G5
13 miles NW of Eastbourne on the A22

Just to the south of Halland lies the interesting and fascinating **Bentley House and Motor Museum**. Covering some 100 acres of beautiful Sussex countryside, the estate cleverly combines a wildfowl reserve, a stately home and a museum in order to provide a fun day out for all the family. Originally a modest 17ᵀᴴ century farmhouse, Bentley was transformed into the splendid Palladian mansion by the architect Raymond Erith who was also behind the restoration of 10, 11 and 12 Downing Street in the 1960s. Exquisitely furnished throughout, the house is particularly renowned for its Chinese Room and the Philip Rickman gallery which contains a collection of over 150 wildfowl watercolours by the celebrated Sussex artist.

The formal gardens surrounding the house are laid out in a series of rooms, separated by yew hedges, and they often follow a colour theme. Beyond are the grounds and a woodland walk through the cool tranquillity of Glyndebourne Wood.

The Motor Museum comprises a superb collection of privately owned vintage cars and motorcycles, many of them roadworthy, which follow the history of motoring from its infancy in the Edwardian era to an elegant modern Lamborghini.

Meanwhile, the waterfowl collection, which includes swans, geese, ducks and flamingos, was begun in the 1960s by the late Gerald Askew. Free to roam in the glorious parkland, the emphasis at the wildfowl centre is on conservation and breeding, particularly of the world's endangered birds. Here, the centre has at least 17 species breeding that are threatened with extinction in the wild.

Set in over three acres of glorious landscaped gardens beside an ancient bluebell wood **Tamberry Hall** is the beautiful, traditional cottage style house that is the home of Rosi and Bob Baynham. Very spacious and bright, this magnificent house was built and superbly decorated and furnished by the couple and only completed in 1998. Though newly built, Tamberry Hall has a comfortable and friendly atmosphere as well as character and charm provided by the extensive use of wooden beams throughout and the large inglenook fireplace. From here

Tamberry Hall, Eastbourne Road, Halland, Lewes, East Sussex BN8 6PS Tel: 01825 880090

the couple offer both bed and breakfast and self catering accommodation. Within the house there are three en suite guest bedrooms, all of which have been carefully fitted with many of the features that are only found in top class hotels -

these include fridges and trouser presses. Guests not only have the opportunity to wander around the splendid garden but also to begin the day with a mouth-watering breakfast served in the dining room and relax in the guest sitting room.

For more privacy, the self catering accommodation is contained in a separate wing of the house and comprises bright and airy living room with dining area, a well equipped kitchen and a large bedroom with spacious bathroom. The ideal place for a holiday base, unfortunately Tamberry Hall is not suitable for children or dogs.

EAST HOATHLY

MAP 2 REF H5

12 miles NW of Eastbourne off the A22

Situated some 20 miles from its namesake, West Hoathly, this compact village was immortalised by Thomas Turner in his *Diary of East Hoathly*. Although the village church was almost completely rebuilt in the mid 19th century, the 15th century squat tower remains from the original building. Known as a Pelham Tower, because it was built by the local Pelham family, the structure has a belt buckle carved on it on either side of the door. This distinctive emblem was awarded to Sir John Pelham for his part in capturing King John of France at Poitiers in 1356.

One of the door emblems has a deep slit in it that was supposedly caused by a bullet fired at Sir Nicholas Pelham in the 17th century. The failed murderer is said to have been a Cavalier, Thomas Lunsford, who joined the French army after being exiled for the attempted murder. He returned to Britain to fight with the king during the Civil War, then emigrated to America and died in Virginia in the 1650s.

Situated on the High Street, just opposite the home of the 18th century diarist Thomas Turner, **Clara's** gift shop and tea rooms occupies a lovely building dating back to the same period. Cheerful and hospitable owner Jane Seabrook offers fine teas and coffees and freshly baked cakes and savouries in warm and cosy country style surroundings. The shop stocks a range of

Clara's, 9 High Street, East Hoathly, East Sussex BN8 6DR Tel: 01825 840339 Fax: 01825 841408 e-mail: claras@netway.co.uk

tasteful antiques, gifts, cards and new and secondhand books, including a volume of Turner's writings on daily life in East Hoathly (1754-1765). Upstairs in the lovely beamed gallery there is a wide range of Rowan knitting yarn for sale and also a fascinating exhibition of traditional knitting and sewing implements.

CHIDDINGLY
MAP 2 REF H5

10½ miles NW of Eastbourne off the A22

This small village is dominated by the tall 15TH century spire of its church, which, at 130 feet is a useful local landmark. Inside the church is a impressive monument to Sir John Jefferay, Baron of the Exchequer under Queen Elizabeth, who lived at nearby Chiddingly Place - a once splendid Tudor mansion that is now in ruins. However, his memorial is overshadowed by that of his daughter and son-in-law, who both appear to be standing on drums. Tradition has it that the Jefferay family once laid a line of cheeses from their manor house to the church door so that they would not get their feet wet. So the large discs of Sussex marble could, in fact, be a reference to those cheeses! Curiously, the monuments have lost hands and fingers over the years as enraged locals knocked them off thinking that the family were related to Judge Jefferies who presided at the Bloody Assize.

Found on what was once the busy London to Eastbourne road, **The Six Bells Inn** was built in the 1730s to cater to the stagecoach travellers. Today, however, though this is a quiet backwater and Jacquie and Paul Newman, the licensees, offer a warm and friendly welcome to locals as well as those walking the nearby Weald Way and the Vanguard Way. An attractive old building that is bedecked with colourful hanging baskets during the summer, there is plenty of comfort-

The Six Bells Inn, Chiddingly, Near Lewes, East Sussex BN8 6HE
Tel: 01825 872227

able seating both inside and in the pleasant patio beer garden. A popular and busy place throughout the year, the cosy interior is separated into several areas: the main bar, with its old brick floor and exposed ceiling beams; the top bar, with piano and inglenook fireplace; and the function room found up a spiral staircase. The village pub atmosphere is added to by the mass of local rugby team memorabilia, farming tools and old posters that adorn all the walls.

Highly regarded for the range of real ales served behind the bar, The Six Bells Inn is also gaining a reputation for the delicious homecooked menu that is served at both lunchtime and in the evening every day. Add to this the live music throughout the week and the Jazz at Sunday lunchtimes and it is easy to see why so many flock here. Finally, the inn has also attracted several ghosts, including a grey cat and the spectre of Sara French who was hanged in Lewes in 1852 after being found guilty of poisoning her husband with arsenic in an onion pie. The jury for the trial, which became known as the Onion Pie Murder, sat in the top bar whilst making their deliberations.

Found in the relaxing and peaceful countryside of the Cuckmere Valley, **Hale Farm House** is surrounded by rolling pasture but it is still within easy reach of the coast, the Wealden Way and Glyndebourne. A wonderful 15th century timber framed farmhouse, Hale Farm has been in David Burrough's family for four generations. David, a Shakespearean actor by profession, and his wife Sue keep riding ponies and have built a large cross country jumping course over the 65 acres of grasslands. From their delightful and historic house, David and

Hale Farm House, Chiddingly, East Sussex BN8 6HQ
Tel & Fax: 01825 872619 e-mail: s.burrough@virgin.net

Sue offer wonderful traditional farmhouse bed and breakfast accommodation in a choice of three guest rooms. A splendid place to stay for those who enjoy the countryside, fresh farm produce for breakfast, and the chance to holiday with their well behaved pets, Hale Farm House has also kept all its old world charm without guests losing out on modern day comforts - the brightly decorated spacious bedrooms contrast with the exposed beams and inglenook fireplaces of the cosy downstairs rooms.

5 The Cinque Ports and the East Sussex Coast

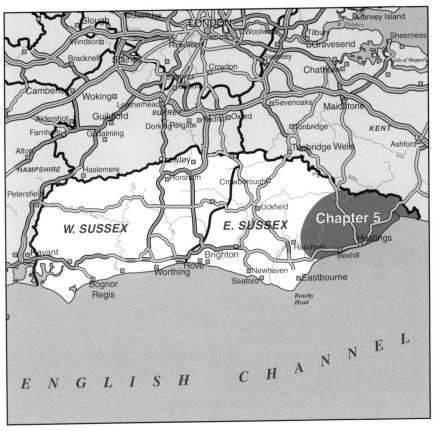

INTRODUCTION

The story of this area of the East Sussex Coast is, of course, that of the events leading up to October 14, 1066. William, Duke of Normandy came here to claim the throne of England and, after defeating Harold a few miles from the town of Hastings, this is exactly what he did. Hastings and Battle, the town that grew up around the abbey that was built on the site of the battlefield, have a concentration of museums and exhibitions on the events of the 11TH century. The victorious Normans soon set about building castles and fortifications from which to defend their new territory and, along with the religious houses that they also founded, this area is rich in the Norman architecture.

As can be seen, the South Coast was susceptible to invasion and, in the days before the Royal Navy, the confederation of Cinque Ports was established to provide a fleet of ships able to defend the coast. Many of the towns that were part of the confederation seem unlikely sources of ships today but the silting up of many of the harbours has changed the landscape of the East Sussex coast considerably in the last 1000 years. More recently, the coast has been the preserve of holiday makers taking advantage of a moderate climate and clean sea air. St Leonards was created in the 1820s and went on to become a fashionable resort whilst the small and more modest Bexhill is home to the impressive modern De La Warr Pavilion that was constructed from steel in the 1930s.

Perhaps though the most picturesque of the coastal towns here is the ancient town of Rye. Situated on a hill and once a great haunt for smugglers, the changing fortunes of the town have left it with a great number of medieval buildings which make it such a charming place to visit.

HASTINGS

Long before William the Conqueror made his landing on the beaches of nearby Pevensey, Hastings was the principal town of a small Saxon province that straddled the county border between Sussex and Kent. Its name comes from 'Haestingas', a Saxon tribal name, and, during the reign of Edward the Confessor, the town was well known for its sailors and ships. In fact, the town became so important that it even had its own mint. Earlier, during the 9TH century, when the Danes were occupying the town, the crowing of a cockerel, awoken by the movements of the townsfolk preparing to surprise their oppressors, alerted the occupying force to the uprising. As a vengeance on all cockerels, the people of Hastings instituted a game called 'cock in the pot', where sticks were thrown at an earthenware pot containing a bird. Whoever threw the stick that broke the pot was given the cock as his prize and the game continued to be played each Shrove Tuesday until the 19TH century.

Following the Battle of Hastings, which actually took place six miles away at Battle, the victorious William returned to Hastings where the Normans began to build their first stone castle in England. Choosing the high ground of West Hill as their site, the massive structure is now in ruins and all that can be seen on the cliff top are the original motte and parts of the curtain wall. However, there are commanding views from here and also the permanent display - **1066 Story at Hastings Castle**. Housed in a medieval siege tent, the exhibition, through clever use of audio-visual techniques, transports visitors back to October 1066.

West Hill also contains a system of elaborate underground passages, known as **St Clement's Cave**, where the naturally formed tunnel network has been extended by man. The caves were leased to Joseph Golding, who spent a great deal of time fashioning the sandstone into sculptures, arcades and galleries and they became one of the town's first commercial sights. Used as air raid shelters during World War II, the caves are now home to the **Smugglers Adventure**, where visitors are told stories of the town's illegal trade by a grizzly old smuggler known as Hairy Jack. After the Conquest, this already important port became a leading Cinque Port, a role it played until the harbour began to silt up in Elizabethan times. Nevertheless, the fishing industry has managed to survive here and today fishing vessels continue to be hoisted on to the shingle beach by a winch. One of the town's greatest features are the tall wooden huts that are used for drying nets and storing fishing tackle. Dating from the 17ᵗ century they are known as net shops or 'deezes'. The old fishermen's church of St Nicholas is now home to the **Fishermen's Museum**, which has, as its centrepiece, *The Enterprise*, one of the last of Hastings' sailing luggers. Also here, amongst the displays of fishing tackle, model boats and historic pictures and photographs, is *The Edward and Mary*, the first locally built boat to have an engine installed. Staying with a maritime theme, there is also the **Shipwreck Heritage Centre**, an award winning museum that is devoted to the history of wrecked ships. Exhibits on display here include a medieval sailing barge sunk on the River Thames in London, the warship, *Anne*, that was beached near Hastings in 1690, and *Primrose*, the last Rye barge. Additional displays concern themselves with modern methods that help eliminate the possibility of a shipwreck, including radar and satellite navigation.

The old part of Hastings consists of a network of narrow streets and alleyways - or "**twittens** - which lie between West and East Hill. There are two cliff railways, one running up each of the hills. West Hill railway runs underground taking passengers to Hastings Castle and St Clement's Caves whilst the **East Hill Railway**, the steepest in England, takes passengers to the cliff top and the beginning of **Hastings Country Park**. This 500 acre park is unlike the cliff tops around Eastbourne as the drop here is not sheer but is split by a series of sloping glens that are over hung with trees. The best way to discover the town's many interesting old residential buildings, inns and churches is to take a walk up the High Street and All Saints Street. **St Clement's Church**, in the High Street, has two cannonballs embedded in its tower, one of which was fired from a French warship, while the **Stag Inn**, in All Saints Street, has a concealed entrance to a smugglers' secret passage and a pair of macabre 400 year old mummified cats.

Occupying the old Town Hall, which was built in 1823, the **Museum of Local History**, is an excellent place to come to for more information on this historic town. Going right back to the Stone Age, and with a considerable section on the Norman Conquest, the museum also covers Hastings' more recent past by including displays on the rise of the Victorian resort, its life as a Napoleonic garrison and its role as a Cinque Port. By contrast, the **Hastings Museum and Art Gallery** covers a wider range of exhibits that also take in the county's ancient crafts. Hastings also contains a variety of attractions that are typical of a traditional seaside resort. The 600 foot long **pier** was completed in 1872 and had to be repaired after World War II when it was deliberately holed in two places to prevent it being used as a landing stage for Hitler's forces. According to local legend, the Conqueror's Stone at the head of the pier was used by William the Conqueror as a dining table for his first meal on English soil. The town also has its own version of the Bayeux Tapestry. Made by the Royal School of Needlework, the **Hastings Embroidery** comprises 27 panels that allow the viewer to walk through all the major events of the last 1000 years. Completed in 1966, among the many scenes and events depicted is the gentleman John Logie Baird - the Scottish pioneer of television who carried out many of his early experiments in Hastings.

AROUND HASTINGS

WESTFIELD
MAP 3 REF J5

3½ miles N of Hastings on the A28

This modern red brick village, on the edge of Brede Level, has, at its old centre, weatherboarded cottages and a Saxon church, with a beautiful Norman arch, that has suffered greatly at the hands of Victorians who added the various internal features.

For a visit with a difference, **Carr Taylor Vineyards** is just the place for anyone interested in the whole winemaking process. Though vineyards in this country are still something of a novelty, Carr Taylor, a family concern, was established, initially on an experimental basis, in 1971 and from then they have gone on to become one of the most highly regarded winemakers in the country. The position of the vineyard is crucial to the success of the business and the gentle rolling slopes of the South Downs are ideal for this southeast facing establishment. Wind breaks help to shelter the crop from the prevailing winds, the high mineral content of the soil is ideal and the vineyard's pioneering work in the development of the high wire trellis system have all added to the establishment and expansion of this highly regarded business. As well as following the Vineyard Trail around the vineyards, where a whole host of traditional English de-

Carr Taylor Vineyards, Wheel Lane,
Westfield, near Hastings,
East Sussex TN35 4SG
Tel: 01424 752501 Fax: 01424 751716

ciduous trees have been added to the hedgerows, visitors are taken around the production side of the business. From the massive presses which crush two tons of grapes in one load, through to the bottling plant, the fascinating process of turning grapes into wine is explained by the friendly and knowledgeable staff. A visit well worth making which finishes in the shop where not only are there wine tastings and refreshments available but also all manner of crafts and gifts.

BREDE

MAP 3 REF J5

5 miles N of Hastings on the A28

Situated to the north of the River Brede, this compact village has a long history that is shrouded in myth and tales of the supernatural. One particular legend is that of the Brede Giant, based around the 16TH century owner of Brede Place, Sir Goddard Oxenbridge. At over seven feet tall he was certainly a giant and, by all accounts, he was a God fearing gentleman of the parish. However, some time after his death stories spread that he was a child eating monster who was eventually killed by a band of Sussex children who, having got him drunk, sawed him in half - the children of East Sussex holding down one end with the children of West Sussex securing the other.

BROAD OAK

MAP 3 REF J5

7 miles N of Hastings on the A28

Just to the north of Brede lies Broad Oak where the attractive and friendly **Rainbow Trout Inn** has a wonderful situation, overlooking the Brede Valley, in this small, quiet village. Originally two cottages, this delightful country pub has

The Rainbow Trout Inn, Broad Oak, Brede, East Sussex TN31 6EU
Tel: 01424 882436

been managed, since 1988, by the very hospitable couple, Trisha and Bob Tyson. As a sponsor of the local village cricket team, this is very much a pub for the local inhabitants but visitors and those holidaying in the area also receive a warm and friendly welcome. As attractive inside as the exterior suggests, there is a cosy and comfortable snug as well as a larger lounge bar but each have the same intimate appeal. Brass and copper jugs and pots hang from the low ceiling beams and the bars serve a range of real ales as well as the usual selection of milds and stouts. In addition, there is a large, separate restaurant, overlooking the pub's garden, where customers can enjoy an extensive menu that includes a wide variety of fish dishes - the house speciality. With the large lawned garden to the side with ample wooden seating for customers, The Rainbow Trout Inn is a pub well worth seeking out.

Tombs of the Oxenbridge family can be seen in the small Norman village church as can a wood carving of the Madonna created by Clare Sherida, a cousin of Sir Winston Churchill who died, aged 84, in 1970. A remarkable woman of her time, she travelled to America where she learnt to carve in wood whilst staying for six months on a Red Indian reservation. In the aftermath of the Russian revolution, she journeyed to Moscow and, staying for two months at the Kremlin, she carved busts of both Lenin and Trotsky.

NORTHIAM
9½ miles N of Hastings on the A28

Map 3 ref J4

This large and picturesque village is known for its characteristic white weatherboarded cottages, some of which, along with a number of fine 17th and 18th century buildings, overlook the triangular green at the heart of Northiam. It was on this green that Elizabeth I is known to have dined and rested in 1573, under a great oak tree, whilst on her journey through Kent and Sussex. Her green high heeled shoes must have been particularly uncomfortable as she took them off here and left them to the villagers who saved them as a memento of her brief visit. Unfortunately, the vast oak tree, which was said to be over 1000 years old and was held together by chains and clamps, has died recently and all that remains on the green is its giant stump.

Of the memorable buildings in the village, **Brickwall House** is one of the finest. This imposing 17th century gentleman's residence was the home of the Frewen family, an old local family who had been living in Northiam since 1573 when the first Frewen came to the village as rector. Well known for its splendid plaster ceilings, there is also a comprehensive series of family portraits which begin in the 17th century. On display in the house are also Elizabeth I's famous green shoes and a sedan chair that belonged to Martha Frewen, who burnt to death in her bedroom in the 1750s. Several members of the family were strict Puritans and one father in particular named his two sons, Accepted and Thankful. Despite the handicap of these unusual names, Accepted went on to become first the president of Magdalen College, Oxford and then the Archbishop of

York, while Thankful is remembered for having donated the communion rails to the church in 1683. The church is also home to an impressive 19th century family mausoleum. Brickwall House, which is so named as it and its grounds are surrounded by a high stone wall, also has as some splendid topiary in the Gardens, as well as an arboretum and chess garden. The house and grounds are open on a limited basis.

Just three miles northwest of Northiam lies **Great Dixter House and Gardens**, one of the finest examples of a late medieval hall house that is surrounded by a very special garden. Built in the 1450s, the manor house was purchased, in 1910, by Nathaniel Lloyd and he then employed Edwin Lutyens to renovate and extend the property. Restoring the house to its original medieval grandeur, as well as adding suitable domestic quarters for an Edwardian household, the Great Hall, which is constructed

Great Dixter House and Gardens

of Wealden oak and was moved here from nearby Benenden to be incorporated into the building, is one of the largest surviving timber framed rooms in the country. Open to the public, many of the original rooms have been filled with antique furniture and examples of 18th century needlework.

However, it is the gardens that make Great Dixter so special. The imaginative design was laid out by Lutyens and, as well as including several existing outbuildings, various new features were added such as the sunken garden, the topiary lawn and the meadow garden. Begun by Nathaniel Lloyd and his wife, Daisy, the gardens were added to by their son Christopher. A regular contributor on gardening to *Country Life*, Christopher's lively and inventive approach to horticulture obviously stems from working in the gardens. A mixture of formal and wild, there are many rare specimens on display here and the gardens are open to the public.

Northiam is also the southern terminal for the **Kent and East Sussex Railway**, which was restored in 1990 and has steam trains running on a track between here and Tenterden in Kent during the summer months. At one time too, the River Rother was navigable to this point and barges were brought upstream to be unloaded at the busy quay. This must have been an ancient port as, in the 1820s, the remains of a Viking long ship were found in the mud by the river where they must have lain since the 9th century.

BODIAM
Map 3 ref J4
10½ miles N of Hastings off the B2244

Situated in the valley of the River Rother, this attractive village, whose name is pronounced 'Bodjem', is home to one of the most romantic castles in the country. In the 1380s, Richard II granted Sir Edward Dalyngrygge a licence to fortify his manor house in order to defend the upper reaches of the then navigable River Rother. Thankfully, Dalyngrygge chose to interpret the licence liberally and one of the last great medieval fortresses in England was built. Construction on **Bodiam Castle** was begun in 1385 when the technology of castle building was at its peak and before the use of gunpowder. Completely surrounded by a wide moat, the arrow slits, cannon ports and aptly named murder holes (through which

Bodiam Castle

objects were thrown at attackers below) were never used in anger. However, there was a minor skirmish here in 1484 and, during the Civil War, the castle surrended without a shot being fired.

A long period of decay followed, during the 17th and 18th centuries, until, in 1829, plans to dismantle the castle were thwarted by 'Mad' Jack Fuller of Brightling. A programme of restoration was begun, firstly by George Cubitt at the end of the 19th century, and completed by Lord Curzon in 1919. On his death in the 1920s, Lord Curzon left the castle to the National Trust and they have continued the restoration programme, including replacing the floors in the towers so that visitors can climb to the top of the battlements and gain a real feel of the security that Bodiam must have offered its inhabitants over the centuries. A popular film location, as the exterior is almost complete, the interior remains somewhat bare.

GUESTLING THORN
4½ miles NE of Hastings on the A259

MAP 3 REF J5

With no real village centre and an isolated ancient church found down a small lane, it is hard now to believe that this was probably the meeting place for the important governing body of the Cinque Ports. However, as it lay on neutral territory and was not controlled by any of the ports, is would have been suitable to the parties concerned.

PETT
4 miles NE of Hastings off the A259

MAP 3 REF J5

Situated on top of a hill the village overlooks, to the south, **Pett Level**, a vast expanse of drained marshland that now consists of watercourses and meadows. Dotted with small lakes the area provides a suitable sanctuary for wildfowl.

The Royal Oak, a charming country inn, has, over the years, had several uses including being a school room - the names of early 19th century school children can still be seen etched on one of the windows - and a village shop before this attractive Grade II listed building became a pub. A traditional place, with a warm and inviting atmosphere, the inn offers visitors a well chosen list of real ales from the bar as well as a full à la carte menu that is supplemented by

The Royal Oak, Pett Road, Pett, near Hastings,
East Sussex TN35 4HG Tel: 01424 812515 Fax: 01424 814733

an ever changing specials menu. Well known for the high quality of the food and ales and for the excellent cellar of wines, it is advisable to book a table at weekends to avoid disappointment. As well as the ample, comfortable and relaxing seating inside this cosy inn, where real fires add extra warmth on cold nights, there is a large lawn to the front of the pub, with an original Victorian post box, and a small and secluded patio area to the rear.

Found down a narrow country lane, **Pendragon Lodge** is a beautifully secluded house in a peaceful rural setting that is truly a hidden place. However, this turn of the century building lies in the heart of the village and it was once Pett's bakery. Today, this attractive house is the home of Dianna Epton who offers superb bed and breakfast accommodation in a choice of three comfortable

Pendragon Lodge, Watermill Lane, Pett, East Sussex TN35 4HY Tel: 01424 814051

en suite guest rooms. Each of the guest rooms has panoramic views over either the well maintained garden surrounding the house or the glorious Sussex countryside and, as with the rest of Pendragon Lodge, the rooms are tastefully furnished and decorated to the highest standard. A delicious breakfast awaits guests each morning which not only includes a full cooked meal but also Dianna's homemade muesli and preserves. In the summer the attractive garden is just the place for quiet contemplation after a day out exploring Sussex and, in an adjoining field, guests can make friends with Dianna's sheep and two angora goats.

Set amid acres of rolling countryside, **Carters Farm Camping and Caravan Park** can be found at the end of a country lane which leads from the village of Pett to the coast. The site is owned and personally managed by brothers, Robert and David Lovejoy, who also run the 177 acre farm

Carters Farm Camping and Caravan Park, Carters Farm, Elm Lane, Pett, near Hastings, East Sussex TN35 4JD Tel: 01424 813206

which specialises in sheep, cattle and cereals. An ideal holiday base for all the family, Carters Farm provides all the usual facilities, including electric hook-ups, showers and daily deliveries of bread and milk. Directly from the attractive and secluded park, there are footpaths to the sea, along the coast and inland to link up with the 1066 Country footpath. There are a number of local pubs, which also serve good food, within walking distance so everyone gets a break on a holiday here. Naturally, with farm animals in close proximity, all dogs should be kept under control and the site is limited to couples and families to ensure that all benefit from the peaceful and relaxing location.

FAIRLIGHT
3 miles NE of Hastings off the A259

MAP 3 REF J5

Separated from Hastings, to the west, by its country park, this village is a small settlement of, chiefly, old coastguard cottages. The 19th century grey stone church occupies a magnificent position overlooking the coast and its tower can be seen for miles out to sea. So much so, in fact, that when the weathervane blew down the villagers were inundated with requests from anxious sailors asking for it to be replaced. In the churchyard, among a surprising number of elaborate tomb-stones, is the rather neglected final resting place of Richard D'Oyly Carte, the founder of the opera company that will be forever linked with Gilbert and Sullivan.

To the west of the village lies **Fairlight Glen**, an attractive place where a gentle stream approaches the sea through a steep side woodland valley. The Lovers' Seat placed here is said to be in memory of a girl who waited on this spot for her lover to return to her from his ship. Unlike many similar tales, this one had a happy ending as, not only did the girl's lover return from overseas un-harmed, but her parents also consented to their marriage.

ST LEONARDS
1 mile W of Hastings on the A259

MAP 3 REF J5

St Leonards was created in the 1820s as a fashionable seaside resort by the cel-ebrated London architect, James Burton, who was responsible for designing much of Bloomsbury. The centrepiece of Burton's plans was the Royal Victoria Hotel, which, although still standing is now rather overshadowed by the vast **Marina Court** that was built to resemble an ocean going liner in the 1930s. Assisted by his son, Decimus, a talented architect in his own right who later designed the Wellington Arch at Hyde Park Corner, London, Burton went on to create a model seaside town that was designed to attract the wealthy and aristocratic.

In its heyday, St Leonard's formal social activities took place in the Assembly Rooms, behind the Royal Victoria Hotel, a classical building that had a tunnel running between the two so that the hotel could provide suitable refreshments for the wide variety of functions. The rooms are now the Masonic Hall. During the Victorian era, this well organised town even had its own services area: Mercatoria was the tradesmen's quarters and Lavatoria the laundrywomen's.

The delightfully informal **St Leonards Gardens** stand a little way back from the seafront and they were originally private gardens maintained by subscriptions from the local residents. Acquired by the local council in 1880, they are a tranquil area of lakes, mature trees and gently sloping lawns that can be enjoyed by everyone.

In the churchyard of the parish church, which was destroyed by a flying bomb in 1944 and rebuilt in a conservative modern style in the 1960s, lies Burton's curious tomb - a pyramid vault where he and several other family members are buried.

Found in a quiet residential street of attractive Victorian town houses, **Rutland Guest House** is a delightful place with views over the seafront and, from rear garden, glimpses of the cliff face. With a magnificent array of colourful hanging baskets and window boxes in the summer and the bright blue awnings over the ground floor windows, this is also an easily recognisable guest house. Owned and personally run by husband and wife, John and Bernie Patterson, the Rutland has a real family air that guarantees that all guests have a relaxing time during their stay here. The guest bedrooms are a mix of sizes to cater for families and single occupancy and, whilst some are

Rutland Guest House, 17 Grosvenor Crescent, St Leonards on Sea, East Sussex TN38 0AA Tel: 01424 714720 Fax: 01424 720379

en suite, all are decorated and furnished to the same high standard as the rest of the guest house. Not only is there a charming, comfortable guest lounge and a separate dining room but everywhere there are an abundance of fresh flowers to really give the place a homely feel. John, generally, prepares the breakfasts and this traditional feast is sure to set everyone up for a full day out exploring the coast and surrounding countryside.

BULVERHYTHE

MAP 3 REF I5

3 miles W of Hastings on the A259

A port during the Middle Ages, in the 19ᵀᴴ century the noise made by the shingle as it was washed by the tide was called the 'Bulverhythe Bells' and their sound was seen as an indicator of bad weather by local fishermen. Just off the coast, at very low tides, the remains of the wreck of the Dutch East Indiaman *Amsterdam* are clearly visible.

BEXHILL

MAP 3 REF I6

5 miles W of Hastings on the A259

This small seaside resort was founded in the 1880s by the influential De La Warr family who lived at the original village of Bexhill, just a mile from the coast. The old Bexhill was an ancient place, with its roots well established in Saxon times when the land around 'Bexlei' was granted to Bishop Oswald of Selsey by Offa, King of Mercia, and for a time it was also a haunt of smugglers. Fortunately a good many of the older buildings have survived the late 19ᵀᴴ century development including old weatherboarded cottages, a 14ᵀᴴ century manor house and the part Norman parish church.

Often referred to as Bexhill-on-Sea, the late 19ᵀᴴ century new resort, though genteel, is rather modest and has never built a pier from the front though there is a promenade and some formal floral gardens. Among the many late Victorian buildings, the **De La Warr Pavilion** certainly stands out. Built in the 1930s by Erich Mendelsohn and Serge Chermayeff, it is a fine and an early example of the functional style of architecture that was becoming fashionable at the time. Looking rather like an ocean going liner, with its welded steel frame, curves, abundance of glass and terraces, the Grade I listed building is now a renowned centre for arts and culture. With a 1000 seater theatre, which attracts many international artists, restaurant, bar and ball room it is very much a focal point of the town.

De La Warr Pavilion

For what would appear today to be a relatively conservative resort, Bexhill was the first seaside town to allow mixed bathing on it beaches - in 1900! A very progressive move then, the gently sloping shingle beaches still offer safe and clean bathing as well as facilities for a range of watersports. The town has another first: in 1902, it played host to the birth of British motor racing when a race and other speed trials were held here. The huge Edwardian cars - nine litres were not uncommon - almost literally flew along the unmade roads around Galley Hill and stopping was a matter of applying the rear wheel brakes, brute force and luck. The anniversary of this first race is celebrated each year in May with the **Bexhill Festival of Motoring**.

To discover more about the history of this seemingly modern but truly ancient settlement a visit to the **Bexhill Museum** is a must. As well as a range of exhibitions on local wildlife, history, geology and archaeology, there are also dinosaurs and even a Great Crab from Japan.

Found in a quiet residential area of the town, yet just 10 minutes stroll from the centre, **Collington Lodge** guest house is a splendid, detached Edwardian house offering comfortable accommodation in a friendly and relaxed atmosphere. A spacious establishment, the guest house is personally run by resident owners, Maureen Shield and David Saunders, who, as pet lovers, are also happy to welcome well behaved pets to their charming house. There are a variety of rooms, from family size to single, but all have been tastefully decorated and furnished in a stylish manner which reflects Maureen's background in

Collington Lodge, 41 Collington Avenue, Bexhill on Sea, East Sussex TN39 3PX Tel & Fax: 01424 210024

textiles. From the rear guest bedrooms there are views out over the sea and, much closer to home, the secluded and well maintained garden. Breakfast is taken in the equally attractive dining room where also, by arrangement, guests can enjoy a homecooked evening meal. Collington Lodge certainly provides an ideal holiday base, in a quiet yet convenient location, guests will also find that the substantial number of local brochures and road maps that Maureen has carefully collected for them to use, a invaluable source of information on where to go and what to see while out discovering the area.

NINFIELD

MAP 3 REF I5

7 miles NW of Hastings on the A269

To the north of this village, straggled along a ridge, lies Ashburnham Place, a red brick house that is much less impressive than it once was. Now in private hands, the house was originally three storeys but there have been many alterations over the years, including the addition of a new block in the 1960s. Meanwhile, the landscaped **Ashburnham Park**, has survived very much on the grand scale in which it was conceived by Capability Brown in the 18TH century though a large number of trees were lost in the hurricane of 1987.

Close to the house lies the **parish church** where, inside, can be found several monuments to the landowning Ashburnham family. One member of the family, John Ashburnham, was a supporter of the monarchy in the Civil War and he followed Charles I on his last journey to the scaffold in London. Imprisoned in the Tower by Cromwell, the late king's possessions that he was wearing on the day of his death - his shirt, underclothes, watch and the sheet in which his body was wrapped - came into the hands of the Ashburnham family. These relics were kept in the church following the restoration of Charles II to the thrown and, for many years, they were believed to offer a cure for scrofula, a glandular disease called King's Evil, to anyone who touched them.

BATTLE

MAP 3 REF I5

6 miles NW of Hastings on the A2100

This historic settlement is, of course, renowned as being the site of the momentous battle, on 14 October 1066, between the armies of Harold, Saxon King of England, and William, Duke of Normandy. The Battle of Hastings actually took place on a hill which the Normans called 'Senlac', meaning 'lake of blood', and even today some believe in the myth that blood seeps from the battlefield after heavy rain. However, any discolouration of the water is, in fact, due to iron oxide present in the subsoil. The battle was a particularly gruesome affair, even for those times, and it was not until late in the afternoon that Harold finally fell on the field - not from an arrow through the eye as is popularly believed but from a series of heavy blows to the head and body which proved fatal. The myth that has grown up around the manner of Harold's death can be traced back to a section of the Bayeux Tapestry where a spear can be seen passing behind Harold's head. This was obviously mistaken for an arrow through his eye and, down the generations, the myth was perpetuated. However, the mystery of Harold's body remains just that. One story tells how it was buried by his mother at Waltham Abbey in Essex while another suggests that William the Conqueror wrapped it in purple cloth and buried it on the cliff top at Hastings.

After the battle and subsequent victory, William set about fulfilling his vow that, if he was victorious, he would build an abbey. Choosing the very spot where Harold fell, **Battle Abbey** was begun straight away and was consecrated in 1094. Throughout the Middle Ages the Benedictine abbey grew increasingly more wealthy and powerful as it extended its influence over wider and wider areas of East Sussex. This period of prosperity, however, came to an abrupt end in 1537 when Henry VIII dissolved the monasteries. The abbey buildings were granted to Sir Anthony Browne and, during a banquet to celebrate his good fortune, a monk is said to have appeared before Sir Anthony announcing that his family would be killed off by fire and water. The prophecy was forgotten as the family flourished until, some 200 years later, in 1793, the home of Sir Anthony's descendant, Cowdray Hall near Midhurst, burnt to the ground. A few days later another member of the family was drowned in the River Rhine in Germany.

Under the custodial care of English Heritage, **Battle Abbey** has much to offer the visitor. The **Prelude to Battle exhibition** introduces visitors to the site and its history. This is followed by a 12-minute video on the Battle of Hastings. Other on-site attractions are a children's themed play and picnic area, an educational Discovery Centre and the recently rediscovered and consecrated **Dunkirk Memorial**, which was placed in the grounds in 1953 by the Men of the Trees organisation. Exciting events are held on a regular basis. Phone 01424 773792 for further details. Open daily 10 a.m.-4 p.m. October-March; 10 a.m.-6 p.m. April-September. Admission is charged.

English Heritage, Battle Abbey, Battle, East Sussex TN33 0AD
Tel: 01424 775705 Fax: 01424 775059

There is more to Battle than the abbey and the battlefield and any stroll around the streets will reveal some interesting buildings. The **Battle Museum of Local History** is an excellent place to discover more about the lives of those living in East Sussex through the ages and there is also a replica of the Bayeux Tapestry to view. Opposite the abbey, and housed in a 600 year old Wealden hall house, is **Buckleys Museum of Shops and Social History**, where more than 50,000 objects are displayed in authentic room settings which cover the period 1850 to 1950. There are even replicas of a Victorian kitchen, a 1930s country railway station and a bicycle shop.

SEDLESCOMBE
Map 3 ref J5

6½ miles NW of Hastings on the B2244

This former flourishing iron founding settlement, is a now a pleasant and pretty village, stretched out along a long sloping green, where the parish pump still stands under a stone building of 1900. The interior of the **village church**, on the northern edge of the village, retains its seating plan of the mid 17TH century which lays out the hierarchy of this rural society in no uncertain terms. The front pew was retained for the Sackville family with the other villagers seated behind. Right at the back, the last few pews were kept for 'Youths and Strangers'.

To the southeast of the village, centred around an adapted 19TH century country house, is the internationally renowned **Pestalozzi Children's Village**. Founded in 1959 to house children from Europe who had been displaced during World War II, the centre follows the theories of the Swiss educational reformer, Johann Heinrich Pestalozzi. The 19TH century Swiss gentlemen, who took into his care orphans from the Napoleonic Wars, believed that young people of all nationalities should learn together. The village now takes children from Third World countries who live here in houses with others from their country under the care of a housemother of the same nationality. After studying for their first degree, the young adults return to their own countries where their newly learnt skills can be put to excellent use in the development of their homelands.

ROBERTSBRIDGE
Map 3 ref I4

10 miles NW of Hastings off the A21

Situated on a hillside overlooking the valley of the River Rother, the village's name is a corruption of *"Rothersbridge"*. In the 12TH century an annexe to a Cistercian Abbey was founded here, by the river, and today some of the buildings can be seen incorporated in a farm. The house's unusually high pitched roof protects the remains of the abbot's house and, in the garden, there are other ruins. Robertsbridge has long been associated with cricket and, in particular, the manufacture of cricket bats. The village establishment of Grey Nicholls has been making bats for many of the sport's famous names, including WG Grace, who, when visiting the village, stayed at The George Inn.

HURST GREEN
Map 3 ref I4

12 miles NW of Hastings of the A21

Set in four acres of gently sloping Weald farmland, close to the village, **Merriments Gardens**, is a place which never fails to delight its visitors. A naturalistic garden, where the deep borders are richly planted according to the prevailing conditions of the landscape, there is an abundance of rare plants here. By contrast, there are also borders that are planted in the traditional manner of an English garden and are colour themed using a mix of trees, shrubs, perennials and grasses. Things change at the gardens all the time, with the seasons and as new ideas are put into operation.

RYE

This old and very picturesque town was originally granted to the Abbey of Fecamp in Normandy, in 1027, and was only reclaimed by Henry III in 1247. It became a member of the confederacy of the Cinque Ports, joining Hastings, Romney, Hythe, Dover and Sandwich as the ports which, before the Royal Navy, were a key part of the south coast's maritime defence and ascended to becoming a full Head Port in the 14th century. Over the years, this hill top town, which overlooks both the Rother estuary and the Romney Marshes, was subjected to many raids, including one by the French in 1377 which left no non stone building still standing. Later, the harbour suffered the same fate as many ports along the south coast as it silted up and the harbour was moved to further down the estuary. **Rye Harbour Nature Reserve**, on the mouth of the River Rother, is a large area of sea, saltmarsh, sand and shingle which supports a wide range of both plant, animal and bird life.

Rye's prominent hill top position was a factor which made it a strategically important town from early times. A substantial perimeter wall was built to defend the northern approaches and one of its four gateways, the **Landgate**, still survives today. This imposing oak structure is all that remains of the fortifications erected by Edward III in the 1340s.

Up a flight of ivy covered steps at the foot of Rye's famous Mermaid Street, the white clapboard façade and striking blue shutters of the **Old Borough Arms** hotel make a welcome sight to any weary traveller. This very pleasant guest house offers excel-

**Old Borough Arms, The Strand, Rye,
East Sussex TN31 7DB Tel & Fax: 01797 222128
e-mail: oldboroughams@btinternet.com**

lent accommodation in a 300 year old former sailors' inn, incorporating part of the 14TH century town wall, constructed to protect Rye from French invaders. Owners Terry and Jane Cox and their daughters Vanessa and Elizabeth have put a bit of themselves into every part of this superb bed and breakfast establishment. The lovely furniture is all handmade by Terry and it is his prized collection of vintage model cars that are on display. The breakfasts are first class, and evening meals are available on prior arrangement (local fish, when available, is a speciality). The flower bedecked patio overlooks Rye's bustling Strand, full of interesting antique shops; the harbour is nearby. The nine en suite rooms in this warm and cosy family run establishment fill up fast - booking is recommended.

Found down a narrow street in the centre of Rye, **The Union Inn** is a charming establishment dating back to the 15TH century that looks for all the world

just what it is: a charming, cosy, and historic town pub. The whitewashed stone walls, casement windows and lanterns that adorn the exterior give a flavour of what is to come. Inside, the atmosphere is relaxed and welcoming. Show cases line the walls, displaying a fine collection of fascinating militaria. There is also a handsome display of finely etched line drawings of RAF Victoria Cross holders. Owner Steve Dartnell is a friendly and diverting host, a fount of interesting and amusing stories, as well as being very knowledgeable on military matters and history. A free house offering a wide choice of beers and also real ales, with an excellent and extensive menu of meals and snacks, The Union is a very

The Union Inn, East Street, Rye, East Sussex TN31 7JY Tel: 01797 222334

popular haunt with locals and visitors alike - booking is essential.

Found in the heart of this ancient town, **Durrant House Hotel** is a charming, spacious Georgian residence that also has a part to play in the history of Rye. Built for a local gentleman in the 17TH century, the house was, like so much of the town, at the centre of the smuggling trade. However, in the 18TH century the property was bought by Sir William Durrant, a friend of the Duke of Wellington, and not only did it then gain its name and its respectability but it was, during the Napoleonic Wars, an operations centre for the defence of the Channel port and a relay station for carrier pigeons bringing news of the victory at Waterloo.

Today, Durrant House is a comfortable town house hotel with character that has been managed by Jo and Ron Kingsland since July 1999. An attractive,

**Durrant House Hotel, 2 Market Street, Rye,
East Sussex TN31 7LA
Tel: 01797 223182 Fax: 01797 226639**

friendly hotel, there is a choice of seven newly furnished and decorated guest rooms, either with en suite or private bathrooms, that guarantee an excellent night's rest. As might be expected, this old building has some interesting features and, as well as the comfortable lounge and separate dining room with it large open fireplace, one of the guest rooms has an unusually curved beam that is said to have come from one of the Armada ships. With views over the River Rother from the rear of the building and the market square to the front, those staying here certainly have the opportunity to gain a real feel of life in Rye.

The town grew prosperous in the late medieval period due to the activities of its fishermen and the merchant fleets that traded with continental Europe. Though the loss of the harbour denied Rye the chief means of earning a living and the town fell into decline visitors today very much benefit from this turn of events as Rye has a large number of medieval buildings remaining which, with more money in the town, would have made way for new structures.

Naturally, being a seafaring town, there are an abundance of old inns and the **Mermaid Inn**, an early timbered building down a cobbled street is one of the most famous. Rebuilt in 1420 after the devastating French raid over 40 years before, the inn was the headquarters of the notorious Hawkhurst Gang in the 18th century. The most infamous band of smugglers on the south coast, in their day, legend has it that they always sat with their pistols close to hand in case of a sudden raid by the excisemen.

Another interesting building is the handsome Georgian residence **Lamb House**, which is now in the hands of the National Trust. Built by a local wine merchant, James Lamb, in 1723 the family were well known in the town and not without a certain amount of influence. Not long after the house was built, the family were involved in Rye's famous murder when, in 1743, a local butcher named Breads killed James Lamb's brother-in-law by mistake. His intention had been to murder James, then the town's Lord Mayor, with whom he held a grudge. Tried and found guilty, Breads was hanged on a gibbet and, there his luck did not change, for his bones were stolen to be used as a cure for rheumatism. Only his skull survives and it can be seen, along with the gibbet, in Rye Town Hall.

More recently, Lamb House, was the home of the novelist, Henry James, who lived here from 1898 to 1916 and many of his personal possessions are on show in the house. James was also responsible for laying out the gardens and he invited many of his friends to the house, including HG Wells, Rudyard Kipling, CK Chesterton and Joseph Conrad. The literary associations do not end there as, in the 1920s, the property was leased to EF Benson who is best remembered for his Mapp and Lucia books which include descriptions of the town that he thinly disguised as 'Tilling'.

Monrow's Bistrot, 14 Cinque Ports Street, Rye, East Sussex TN31 7AD Tel & Fax: 01797 224294

The modest front of **Monrow's Bistrot**, in the heart of Rye, hides a charming and delightful French restaurant that is managed by mother and son, Kate and Jamie. Kate was born in Finistere, France, and gained her early cooking experience from her Bordeaux born grandmother and, whilst she is busy creating the delicious dishes, Jamie is taking care of the customers. Small and intimate, this is very much a French style bistrot - here spelt the French way - with soft lighting, candles on the tables, and a friendly and relaxed atmosphere. The restaurant's previous owner, Irene, not only named the place, after Marilyn Monroe whose pictures adorn the walls, but also started the French theme which continues today. Since taking over, Kate and Jamie have expanded the menu, which changes daily, and they have introduced more sea food as well as game and, in particular, duck which is a Monrow's speciality. Beautifully prepared and presented, there is a wonderful five course set menu which includes an outstanding cheeseboard, that is sure to have everyone's mouth watering.

One of Rye's oldest surviving buildings is **Ypres Tower** which forms part of the **Rye Castle Museum**, the other part being in East Street. The collection concentrates on the town's varied past and includes exhibitions on smuggling, law and order and the iron industry. Meanwhile on the second site, there is an old fire engine, pottery made in the town, nautical equipment and much more that makes up the full history of Rye. Combining the traditional craft of model making with the latest electronic techniques, the **Rye Heritage Centre** presents a model of the town, complete with light and sound, that transports visitors back through the ages.

Found tucked away in the streets below Ypres Tower, **The Ypres Inn** - known locally as The Wipers due to the English inability to pronounce French - is an attractive timber clad building dating from the 17th century. The first landlord, in 1663, was Mr Bourn and his 7th generation grandson still uses the inn. Today, this well known inn is personally managed by Babs and Dick Pearce, a warm and friendly couple who have certainly put The Ypres on the map. As well as serving a range of real ales, in-cluding a local micro brewery ale, and the usual beers, lagers, and ciders, visitors to the inn are treated to a mouthwatering menu of tradition pub food and also Dick's speciality lamb dishes. All the meals, from the sand-wiches and baguettes to the splendid Sunday carvery, are freshly prepared and homecooked. Customers too can take part in a number of tradi-tional pub games, including darts, cribbage, and dominoes, whilst the more energetic may like to try their hand at The Ypres' most popular game, petanque, which is played in the garden opposite the pub. How-ever, it is as a blues pub that The Ypres is particularly well known. Live music (always blues) is played here each Sunday evening

The Ypres Inn, Gun Garden, Rye, East Sussex TN31 7HH Tel: 01797 223248 Fax: 01797 227460

and the groups and players here have drawn keen music fans from both near and far.

While in the High Street, the pretty crimson coloured doorway with its panes of multicoloured glass above the frontage tells visitors that they have arrived at

Cranberries of Rye, one of the town's most distinguished tea rooms. Open seven days a week for morning tea or coffee, a light lunch, or traditional cream tea, this very welcoming establishment is run with enthusiasm by owners Hilary and Ray Jones. All cakes on the menu are homemade - some to customers' orders: scones, tea cakes, pastries, fruit cake, lemon cake, treacle tart, chocolate cake and meringues are just some of the delectables on offer, as well as soups, fresh breads and fresh or toasted sandwiches with a choice of fillings. To accompany these delicious comestibles there is an excellent choice of coffees

Cranberries of Rye, 105A High Street, Rye, East Sussex TN31 7JE Tel: 01797 224800

and teas, as well as fruited teas, soft drinks, and hot chocolate. Jams, marmalades, pickles, chutneys, honeys, and cordials are on sale, as well as good quality handmade teapots.

River Rother at Rye

Originally two cottages which belonged to Leneys Dover Brewery, **Wish House** is a wonderful Grade II listed building dating from around 1800 that is now the home of Rowena and Paul Sterry. A charming house which, like many in the area, has peg tiles on the walls, the couple first opened their home to bed and breakfast customers in 1997 and it has proved a great success. There are two spacious en suite guest rooms that have been stylishly decorated and furnished

Wish House, Wish Ward, Rye, East Sussex TN31 7DH
Tel: 01797 223672

with guest's comfort very much in mind. Each overlooks the splendid and secluded walled garden where, weather permitting, breakfast is served on the patio. For the evenings, guests can settle down for a quiet read or conversation in the guest lounge, which has the added comfort of an open log burning fire on chilly nights. This friendly professional couple take every care to ensure that everyone has a wonderful stay here and, as well as serving a delicious homecooked breakfast, with homemade preserves, dinner is also available.

Lying within Rye's conservation area, **The Mill Restaurant** can be found in a wonderful old building that dates back to around 1760. This large sandstone warehouse, overlooking the River Tillingham, originally stored provisions for the town but, by the late 1800s, it was used as a working mill, grinding grain for the local corn merchants. Though many of the buildings structural features remain, the only evidence of the restaurant's past life is the wooden drive wheel that has pride of place behind the bar. As might be expected, this is a spacious and interesting restaurant but it is also a relaxed place with a convivial atmosphere that makes for leisurely dining. Managed by the experience Brian Smith, this restaurant has a fine reputation for the high standard of its cuisine and the

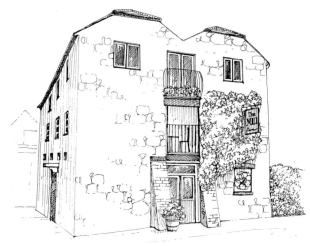

pleasant ambience and professional service go to make this an excellent choice for a memorable meal. At the heart of The Mill Restaurant's success is the carefully selected fresh local produce that goes into their interesting and varied menu. Local fish features heavily and each dish is prepared in such a manner as to compliment the full flavour of the fish. However, the stylish surroundings

The Mill Restaurant, Strand Quay, Rye, East Sussex
TN31 7DB Tel: 01797 224995

and the superb cuisine is not all that is on offer to the customer here as the restaurant is also gaining a reputation for the regular live jazz evenings held here. A popular place, it is necessary to book here, particularly during the season.

Situated just outside the town, **The Top o' the Hill** is an attractive family run inn that combines style and sophistication with a warm and relaxed atmos-

The Top o' the Hill, Rye Hill, Rye, East Sussex TN31 7NH
Tel: 01797 223284 Fax: 01797 227030

phere. The building dates from the 17th century and it probably became a pub in the 1800s when it served the needs of those travelling what was then a main highway just outside the door. Now run by Shirley and Gerry Manklow, with the help of their daughter, Jo, this friendly establishment provides both locals and visitors to Rye with superb hospitality. Very much decorated in a style that befits a building of this age, the pub area is welcoming and intimate and here customers can enjoy a range of real ales as well as the usual beers, ales and lagers. There are two dining areas, one in the old building and the other, surprisingly, in a recent extension, though its looks as though it has been here for centuries. The kitchen is Shirley's area of expertise and, along with her delicious homemade pies, there is a mouthwatering menu of traditional English food available with a fine accompanying wine list. However, the hospitality does not end there as The Top o' the Hill can also offer customers the choice of eight charming en suite guest rooms in a splendid cottage style annex.

Culpeppers, a name steeped in Sussex history, is built on a former orchard, adjacent to farmland and river paths and yet within a few minutes walk of the town centre. South facing and situated down a quiet cul de sac, this spacious modern and comfortably furnished home also has a delightful and unusual Mediterranean style terraced garden which gives excellent views of the town and the surrounding countryside. A guest home, run by owners Pat and John Ciccone, Pat welcomes all guests with tea and biscuits or homemade cake in the friendly surroundings of the kitchen before showing them to the charming guest

Culpeppers, Love Lane, Rye, East Sussex TN31 7NE
Tel & Fax: 01797 224411 e-mail: peppersrye@aol.com
website: www.rye-tourism.co.uk/culpeppers

rooms. There are three - two singles which overlook the fields opposite the house and a twin en suite room with a small balcony overlooking the terraced garden. All offer a comfortable and pleasant place to use as a holiday base and Pat and John certainly aim to make every guest's stay as comfortable as possible. There is also a guest lounge, the perfect place in which to relax, where the couple have a ready supply of information about the local area as well as a selection of novels, games and puzzles. Guests too are encouraged to make use of the garden, with its large summer house and views.

AROUND RYE

PLAYDEN
MAP 3 REF K4
1 mile N of Rye off the A268

This smart hamlet has a rather battered old **12**TH **century church**, with a shingle broach spire, that has inside an unusual memorial to a 16TH century Flemish brewer. A refugee from Spanish persecution in the Low Countries, Cornelis Roetmans settled in the area along with a community of Huguenots. He carried on his trade as brewer and, after his death, he was remembered in the church by a memorial slab that is carved with beer barrels and mash forks - the tools of his trade.

The country lanes to the northeast of Playden lead to the start of the **Royal Military Canal**, an unusual waterway that was built in 1804 as part of the defences against a possible invasion by Napoleon. There is a 20 mile long towpath between Rye and Hythe which offers easy and attractive walking along the fringes of the now drained **Walland** and **Romney Marshes**.

CAMBER
MAP 3 REF K5
3 miles SE of Rye off the A259

The village has seen a lot of development since World War II with the building of bungalows on the sand dunes. However, though the appearance is relatively modern, Camber is also home to **Camber Castle**, a fine example of a series of coastal defences built by Henry VIII in the 16TH century. Now in the hands of English Heritage, the fortress seems rather far inland today (due to the receding tides) though, when it was built, it held a commanding position on a spit of land on one side of the Rother estuary.

WINCHELSEA
MAP 3 REF J5
2½ miles SW of Rye on the A259

Though Winchelsea lies only a short distance from Rye, there could be no greater contrast: whilst Rye is a place of tourist bustle, Winchelsea is a quiet place that time seems to have forgotten. An ancient Cinque Port and the smallest town in

England, until the 13ᵀᴴ century Winchelsea lay several miles to the south on a site which was eventually engulfed by the sea after a series of violent storms. The 'new' Winchelsea stands on a hill and it was built to a rigid grid pattern laid out by Edward I. The ambitious rectangular plan of 39 squares - a feature which can still be seen some 700 years later - became the home of some 6000 inhabitants which is nearly 10 times the number of residents today.

For a short time in the 14ᵀᴴ century Winchelsea prospered as the most important Channel port but again nature took its toll and the town lost its harbour. The port went into decline and, along with the Black Death and constant raids by the French, the town fell into almost complete obscurity. It was not until the mid 19ᵀᴴ century that a successful recovery plan was put together to restore the town to something like its former grandeur and historic beauty. **Winchelsea Court Hall Museum** illustrates the events that led to the town's prosperity, culminating in it being made a Head Port of the confederation of Cinque Ports, and then its gradual decline. The museum is housed in one of Winchelsea's oldest surviving buildings and, close by, can be seen the ruins of a 14ᵀᴴ century **Franciscan Friary**.

Today, Winchelsea has a special atmosphere that is all its own and, throughout the 20ᵀᴴ century, artists and writers have been attracted to the place.

BECKLEY   MAP 3 REF J5
4½ miles NW of Rye on the B2088

When Alfred the Great died in 900, he referred to lands at 'Beccanleah' in his will and there was certainly a Saxon church here though a more modern building stands on the site. A medieval building with a Norman tower, inside there are two grotesque stone heads with leaves protruding from the mouths that were known as 'jack in the greens'. On still nights, it is said that Sir Reginald Fitzurse can be heard riding furiously to the church for sanctuary after taking part in the murder of Thomas à Becket.

The Royal Oak Inn is an interesting old building in that the front dates from the 1830s whilst the back of the inn was originally two cottages built in around 1650. Hard to miss, the pub, which is thought to have once been a Victorian workhouse, stands back from the road and its large front façade is bedecked with flower filled hanging baskets in the summer. Owned and personally run by Maureen and Martyn, this friendly and inviting inn offers a warm welcome to both locals and visitors alike. As well as the central wooden bar area, there is a quiet and comfortable library end, with shelves of books for customers to read if they wish, and a charming and intimate restaurant area. Evidence of Martyn's previous career, as a London fireman, can be seen all over the pub's interior as the memorabilia all relates to the fire service and there are some impressive old fire insurance marks. Well known and highly regarded for the excellent range of real ales found behind the bar, The Royal Oak is also just

The Royal Oak Inn, Main Street, Beckley, East Sussex TN31 6RJ
Tel: 01797 260312

the place for a delicious homemade meal. Fish is certainly order of the day on Fridays whilst the traditional Sunday roast lunches are always popular.

Jenny Farrant and her son Paul are in partnership running the superb **Farm World** in Beckley. Beginning as a children's farm in 1984, it now offers a range of interesting sights and experiences for children of all ages. It has become a popular attraction for locals and visitors alike, with a range of farm animals and offering an insight into traditional and modern farming methods. Located at Great Knelle

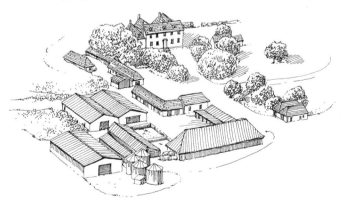

Farm World, Great Knelle Farm, Beckley, nr Rye,
East Sussex TN31 6UB Tel: 01797 260250/260321

Farm, set amid 600 acres of peaceful countryside, including woodland and a stretch of the River Rother, the farm makes a lovely day out for all the family. Other exciting and informative features include two miles of trails suitable for walkers of all levels, and fishing on the river. Also onsite is a charming letting cottage which sleeps four. The perfect rural retreat, with every amenity and where guests are ensured a friendly and hospitable welcome, Farm World is well worth a visit.

6 Ashdown Forest and the Sussex Weald

INTRODUCTION

This region of East Sussex, centred around the ancient Ashdown Forest - a royal hunting ground that also provided the fuel for the area's iron industry - is characterised by small towns and villages of weatherboarded cottages, traditional hall houses and unspoilt farms. Much of the actual woodland has been lost both as fuel and for shipbuilding. Though the area has been inhabited from ancient times, the discovery of a supposedly 150,000 year old skull in 1912 at the village of Piltdown caused much excitement but it proved to be a hoax some 40 years later.

Over the centuries there have been many fine houses and castles in the area and, in particular, there is the still impressive Herstmonceux Castle. Home of the Royal Observatory from 1948 until the 1980s, this magnificent medieval brick fortress, which also provided comfortable living accommodation for its inhabitants, is set in glorious gardens and parkland.

Other houses here have a more personal appeal and one, Bateman's at Burwash, was the home of Rudyard Kipling from 1902 until his death in 1936. A quiet place in a secluded position, the house has been left as it was when Kipling died and is full of his personal possessions. Ashdown Forest and Hartfield are linked with another 20th century novelist - AA Milne. He lived close by and wrote the Winnie the Pooh stories, which were set in the forest and surrounding area, for his son Christopher Robin.

CROWBOROUGH

This Wealden town, on the eastern edge of Ashdown Forest, is, at over 750 feet above sea level, one of the highest towns in Sussex. Before the arrival of the railways, in the 1860s, this was a small community of iron smelters and brigands centred around the parish church and vicarage which dates from the 18th century. However, the railways put Crowborough within easy reach of London and it was gradually transformed into a flourishing residential town. This theme continues today as Crowborough not only has good shopping and recreational facilities but also pleasant modern housing.

Situated down a quiet cul de sac, **Bryher Patch** is the attractive home of Rosemary and Bryan Cowling who moved here just four months after the house was built in 1982. With an attractive lawned front garden and a secluded terraced rear garden outlined with pine trees and a mature lime tree, this really is a delightful and peaceful setting. Since 1989, Rosemary and Bryan have been providing excellent bed and breakfast accommodation

**Bryher Patch, 18 Hydehurst Close, Crowborough,
East Sussex TN6 1EN Tel: 01892 663038**

from their charming house and, as a measure of their success, they receive many return guests. There are two comfortable letting rooms, one twin and one double, which both overlook the rear garden and, as they share the same bathroom, it is usually to friends or to families that the rooms are let, although single occupancy is always welcome. Breakfast is very much seen as a meal to set guests up for their day ahead and special requirements are happily catered for. When Rosemary is not busy looking after her guests she finds time to create the wonderful decoupage that can be seen all around the house. For anyone still guessing, the house's name is derived from Bry - Bryan - and Her - her indoors!

On the highest place in Crowborough stands **Beacon House** which, though only built in 1838, is one of the town's oldest buildings. At the heart of the town is a triangular green, where can be found another ancient, by Crowborough standards, building - the grey stone classical church which dates from 1744. Though a relatively uneventful place, its convenient location meant that the town attracted a number of well known late 19TH century writers and, in particular, Sir Arthur Conan Doyle, creator of Sherlock Holmes.

AROUND CROWBOROUGH

BOARSHEAD
1½ miles NE of Crowborough on the A A26

MAP 2 REF H4

Found in the heart of the attractive village of Boarshead, just northeast of Crowborough, **The Boars Head Inn** is a quintessential English country pub

The Boars Head Inn, Boarshead, Near Crowborough,
East Sussex TN6 3HD Tel: 01892 652412 Fax: 01892 665523
e-mail: gordon@cheerful.com

that offers both locals and visitors the very best in hospitality as well as pleasant and peaceful surroundings. The inn building has been traced back, through archives, to have been built in the 17th century and, though times have changed, The Boars Head remains typically English. The bar area and the separate, intimate dining area have both retained their exposed ceiling beams and each has a wonderful stone inglenook fireplace, with a boar's head above, that is lit in the winter months. As well as the beams, there is wood everywhere - the floors, wood clad walls and tables and chairs - and all have been highly polished to bring out the rich, deep colours. Famous locally for the delicious meals that are served here in both the dining room and in the light and airy garden room, owners, Jill and Gordon McKenzie, have a fine reputation for their homemade choice of dishes. The menu changes constantly and, as well as the special meals for Valentine's Day and Mothering Sunday, booking is also advisable for the very popular Sunday roast lunches. However, this charming inn is also the place for an excellent pint of ale - there is always a good selection of real ales - beer or lager and, when the weather is fine, customers can made use of the rear patio garden overlooking the new Boars Head Golf Centre or the lawned gardens to the front of the building.

GROOMBRIDGE

Map 2 ref H3

4 miles N of Crowborough on the B2110

This unspoilt village straddles the county border with Kent and, whilst the Sussex part of the village, which grew up around the railway station has little to offer, the Kent side is particularly charming. Centred around a triangular green, there are attractive 15th and 16th century estate cottages and a superb manor house. **Groombridge Place** - the name is said to be derived from the Saxon 'Gromen', meaning man as in bridegroom - and it dates from the 17th century. However, the site on which the foundations were laid is much older and there is some evidence that there was first a Saxon then a Norman castle here. Built by Charles Packer, the Clerk of the Privy Seal, who accompanied Charles I on his unsuccessful journey to Spain to ask for the Infanta's hand in marriage, it is a splendid red brick house surrounded by a moat. Set within beautiful terraced gardens (which are occasionally open to the public), when seen it is not surprising that the surrounding woodland has been dubbed the Enchanted Forest. It was also Charles Packer who, as a staunch Protestant, had the chapel built in thanks that the king's mission to Spain failed.

HADLOW DOWN

Map 2 ref H4

4 miles SE of Crowborough on the A272

This handsome hamlet is surrounded by undulating lanes that weave their way through some of the most glorious Wealden countryside. Just outside Hadlow Down is the **Wilderness Wood**, a unique family run woodland that does much to maintain the crafts and techniques of woodland management. Visitors can see the woodland being tended in the traditional chestnut coppices and plantations of pine, beech and fir. The wood is then harvested and the timber fashioned, using traditional techniques, into all manner of implements in the centre's workshops. This is very much a living museum of woodland management and, for many, a real eyeopener that is well worth seeing. There are also woodland trails, a bluebell walk and an adventure playground.

WALDRON
7 miles S of Crowborough off the B2192

MAP 2 REF H5

The 13TH century village **church of All Saints** has a lovely kingpost roof and, unusually for its age, a very wide aisle and nave the reason for which has never quite been explained.

Found in the heart of the village, along with the church and the war memorial, is **The Star Inn Waldron**, a splendid old freehouse that dates back to 1620. This is everything a village pub should be - a place to catch up on the local news and a place to enjoy fine hospitality. With seating under colourful hanging baskets at the front and a large lawned garden with further seating, this is a lovely establishment for a summer day but the interior is equally inviting. The

The Star Inn Waldron, Waldron, near Heathfield,
East Sussex TN21 0RA Tel: 01435 812495

main bar area has cosy wood panelling, a large inglenook fireplace (the fire plate of which is dated 1694) and a mass of pictures of Waldron in days gone by which together give the inn its traditional air. Here customers can enjoy a pint or two from the excellent selection of regularly changing real ales on offer which includes the local favourite Harveys. Hosts, Paul and Lesley Lefort, along with their three children Amie, William and George, also welcome customers to try something from either the lunchtime menu or the evening à la carte. Both are a real treat and offer a tasty mix of traditional pub food along with some interesting and mouthwatering alternatives that are sure to please everyone. Taken in the bar or in the equally charming separate dining room, where an old fashioned mangle has pride of place, a Star Inn homecooked meal is well worth travelling to enjoy.

Situated on the edge of the village and surrounded by its quiet and secluded cottage garden lies **Barns Oak**, a charming small country house. This attractive house has been the home of Jane Davenport-Thomas since 1993 and, from 1997, she has been offering wonderful bed and breakfast accommodation in two delightful twin rooms. Each is beautifully decorated and furnished and guests can not only enjoy the comforts of the house but also the glorious garden with fields beyond. Jane trained as a florist and now runs her business from

**Barns Oak, Firgrove Road, Waldron, near Heathfield,
East Sussex TN21 0RE Tel & Fax: 01435 864574**

home and there are fresh flowers and plants dotted all around the house. Those coming here should also be fond of animals as Jane has two friendly dogs, three cats and, housed in the small adjoining stable block five horses and ponies. Barns Oak is a no smoking establishment and it is not suitable for children under 10.

BUXTED
MAP 2 REF G4
5 miles SW of Crowborough on the A272

This village, in more ways than one, has been dominated by the great house of **Buxted Park** (which is still privately owned). The present house was built along classical lines in 1725, though it was nearly destroyed by fire in 1940. Then in the hands of architect Basil Ionides, its has been much altered from its original design and various items, including the main staircase and front door, actually came from other buildings. In the 19ᵀᴴ century the house was the home of Lord Liverpool and, wishing to give himself more privacy, the noble earl decided to move the village further away. The villagers were incensed and refused to move so, reaching a stalemate, Lord Liverpool declined to repair their estate cottages.

Eventually the villagers gave way and moved to the rather ordinary village that is now Buxted. However, several buildings have remained in the old location including, at the entrance to the park gates, the half timbered **Hogge House**. Dating back to the 16ᵀᴴ century, the house was once the home of Ralph Hogge (though some believe his name to have been Huggett) who is said to have been the first man to cast guns in England in 1543. The much restored 13ᵀᴴ century parish church also remains in the park's grounds and the Jacobean pulpit was once used by William Wordsworth's brother who was vicar here for a time.

MARESFIELD
MAP 2 REF G4

5½ miles SW of Crowborough off the A22

Before the turnpikes between London and the south coast were laid through the Weald, this was a remote place but the 18ᵀᴴ century saw the development of Maresfield as it stood at a crossroads. The tall Georgian Chequers Inn is arguably the village's oldest building and a fine example of a coaching inn. Close by is an white painted iron milestone with the 41 and four bells and bows in outline. One of a whole chain of such milestones that stood on the old turnpike road, this is a particularly witty one as it refers to the distance, in miles, from Maresfield to Bow Bells, London.

PILTDOWN
MAP 2 REF G4

7½ miles SW of Crowborough off the A272

Though the village is not generally known to many, its name is famous, particularly in academic circles. In 1912, an ancient skull was discovered by the Lewes solicitor and amateur archaeologist, Charles Dawson, in the grounds of Barcombe Manor. At the time, archaeologists the world over were looking for a 'missing link' between man and the ape and the skull seemed to fit the bill - it had a human braincase and an ape like jaw. Believed to be about 150,000 years old it was not until the 1950s, and with much improved scientific dating techniques, that the skull was proved to be a fake. It was, in fact, the braincase of a medieval man who had suffered a bone thickening disease and the jaw of an orang-utan. The perpetrator of the hoax was never discovered. It certainly could have been Dawson himself but various other theories have been put forward including one which points to Sir Arthur Conan Doyle, the author of the Sherlock Holmes stories and a well known Christian fundamentalist.

Though the skull has been proved a hoax, the village inn, which changed its name to the **Piltdown Man** in 1912 still carries the name and an inn sign with the famous skull on one side and a stone carrying humanoid on the other.

UCKFIELD
MAP 2 REF G5

7 miles SW of Crowborough on the B2102

Situated in the woodland of the Weald, on the River Uck, this was once a small village at the intersection of the London to Brighton turnpike road with an ancient pilgrims' way between Canterbury and Winchester. Before the stage coaches arrived and a number of coaching inns sprang up, this was, due to its position - close to woods and water - a centre of the iron industry. However, despite these advantages, Uckfield remained small until the 19TH century, when a period of rapid expansion followed the arrival of the railway.

Several of the old coaching inns survived the move from horsedrawn to steam powered travel and, amongst the Victorian buildings, lies **Bridge Cottage**, a fine example of a medieval hall house.

SHEFFIELD GREEN
MAP 2 REF G4

8 miles SW of Crowborough on the A275

The village takes its name from the manor house, a Tudor building that was remodelled in the 1770s by James Wyatt for the John Baker Holroyd, MP, the 1ST Earl of Sheffield. At the same time as creating his mansion, **Sheffield Park**, the earl had Capability Brown landscape the gardens. During his time here, the earl's great friend, Edward Gibbon, came to stay during the last months of his life and it was while here that he wrote much of his epic *Decline and Fall of the Roman Empire* in the library.

A later inhabitant, the 3RD Earl of Sheffield, was a keen cricketer and was the first to organise the test tours between England and Aus-

Sheffield Park Gardens

tralia. At the same time he began a tradition (which lasted until a short time ago) that the visiting team came to Sheffield Park to play their first match against the Earl of Sheffield's XI. Though the house remains in private hands, the splendid **Gardens** are open to the public and from the mass of daffodils and bluebells in spring to the blaze of colour from the rare trees and shrubs in autumn there is plenty to look at and enjoy.

Not far from the house, in the village, lies the **Sheffield Arms**, a coaching inn that was built by the 1ˢᵀ Earl in the 18ᵀᴴ century. Local stories told of a cave behind the inn with an underground passageway to a nearby farmhouse that was used by smugglers and, in order to test out the truth of the tales, three ducks were shut into the cave. After 10 days, one of the ducks reappeared - in the cellars of the farmhouse.

The village is also the terminus of the **Bluebell Railway** and the cricketing earl would surely have been pleased with the railway's success today as he was on the board of the Lewes and East Grinstead Railway that originally built the line. The other terminus can be found near East Grinstead.

CHAILEY
MAP 2 REF G5
9 miles SW of Crowborough on the A275

This large and scattered parish comprises three villages: North Chailey, Chailey

and South Common. Though small, Chailey has some impressive old buildings including the 13ᵀᴴ century parish church and a moated rectory. To the north, lies **Chailey Common**, a nature reserve covering some 450 acres of wet and dry heathland where also can be found **Chailey Windmill**. Unlike many Sussex windmills, Chailey's splendid smock mill was saved from ruin just in time.

Overlooking the common is **Chailey Heritage**, which was founded in 1903 as a home for boys with tuberculosis from the East End of London. As treatments for the now less prevalent disease have progressed, the home has become a learning centre for children with disabilities and has a world wide reputation.

Chailey Windmill

NEWICK
Map 2 ref G4

9 miles SW of Crowborough on the A272

The village is centred around its large green on which stands an unusual long handled pump that was erected to mark Queen Victoria's Diamond Jubilee in 1897. The actor, Dirk Bogarde, was brought up in the area and was given his first big part in an amateur production here in the 1930s.

NUTLEY
Map 2 ref G4

5 miles SW of Crowborough on the A22

The village is home to **Nutley Windmill**, Sussex's oldest working windmill. It was restored in 1968 by a group of enthusiasts after it had stood unused and neglected from the turn of the century.

For a taste of real Indian cuisine, the **Ganges Restaurant** is a well known and highly regarded restaurant that has an excellent reputation for maintaining the traditions of Indian cooking that have developed over thousands of years. First opened in 1988 by Khaled Mannan and his two other partners, the Ganges has gone from strength to strength. A modern and distinctive building, the interior is opulent without being overbearing and, with silver tableware, crisp white linen and a splendid central indoor fountain, the experience of dining

Ganges Restaurant, Nutley High Street, Nutley, East Sussex TN22 3NG Tel: 01825 713287

here does not begin and end with the food. The menu, which changes regularly, offers a comprehensive selection of Indian dishes that includes all the famous recipes from India's many diverse regions. Specialising in wild duck and fresh water fish, as well as their famous Tandoori cuisine that is prepared in a traditional clay oven, choosing a meal here is an interesting and enjoyable experience. However, for those who find themselves lost, the helpful and knowledgeable staff are always on hand to suggest suitable dishes. Open seven days a week for both lunch and dinner and also with a takeaway service, the Ganges Restaurant is well worth taking the time to visit.

ASHDOWN FOREST
MAP 2 REF HG4

3 miles W of Crowborough on the B2026

This ancient tract of sandy heathland and woodland on the high ridges of the Weald is the largest area in southeast England that has never been ploughed and put to agricultural use. The original meaning of 'forest' was as a royal hunting ground and this is exactly what Ashdown Forest was. The earliest record dates from 1268 and its thriving population of deer made it a particularly favourite sporting place. However, the area was used long before this and, in prehistoric times, there was a network of trackways across the forest. Later, the Romans built a road straight across it and, by the time of the Norman invasion, the rights of the commoners living on its fringes, to gather wood for fuel, cut peat and graze cattle, were well established.

During medieval times it was a great place for sport and a 'pale', or ditch, was dug around it to maintain the deer within its confines. A famous sporting owner was John of Gaunt, the Duke of Lancaster and during his ownership the forest became known as Lancaster Great Park. Henry VIII and James I were also frequent visitors. However, by the end of the 15TH century much of the woodland had gone, as fuel for the area's iron industry and, during the chaos of the Civil War, the forest was neglected and, by 1657, no deer remained.

Today, the forest is a place of recreation with many picnic areas and scenic viewpoints through there are few public footpaths. The deer have returned and the clumps of Scotch pines that make prominent landmarks on the higher points were planted in the 19TH century.

WYCH CROSS
MAP 2 REF G4

6 miles W of Crowborough on the A275

Marking the western limit of Ashdown Forest, local folklore has it that the village's name is derived from a cross that was erected on the spot where the body of Richard de Wyche, Bishop of Chichester, was rested overnight on the journey from Kent to its burial place in Chichester during the 13TH century.

FOREST ROW
MAP 2 REF G4

6 miles NW of Crowborough on the A22

This hillside village in Ashdown Forest is a popular place with walkers and also a good starting point for wonderful forest drives. The village was founded in the late Middle Ages when the forest was still extremely dense in places and provided a thick swathe of vegetation between the Thames valley and the south coast.

Unusually many of the village's buildings are older than the parish church which only dates from 1836. The village is also the proud owner of a stone wall which commemorates a visit made by President John F Kennedy.

The Swan Hotel, in the heart of Forest Row, is a pub that is well worth taking the time to find. Managed by experienced local licensees, Sandra and Ernest Wright, the oldest parts of this inn are medieval when the establishment served as an ale house to drovers, packhorse men and smugglers. Today's buildings date from the 18TH and 19TH centuries when, then called The Yew Tree, the pub became a busy coaching inn on the turnpike road between London and Brighton. The age and history of this splendid pub can be seen in the interior decoration of this friendly and relaxing place. With large log burning fireplaces,

**The Swan Hotel, Lewes Road, Forest Row,
East Sussex RH18 5ER Tel: 01342 822318**

low beamed ceilings, a cosy intimate snug and a large separate games room, there is also plenty of space here for those who have already discovered the delights of The Swan. As well as the excellent menu of traditional bar snacks and meals, there is a comprehensive wine list and an range of real ales, beers and lagers served behind the bar. A lively place at the weekends, when there is also live music on a regular basis, The Swan has a large garden, with a patio and lawn, that makes it ideal on warm summer days.

Found next to Chequers Hotel is **Village Crafts**, a wonderful Aladdin's cave dedicated to all manner of crafts and skills that is the brainchild of owner Jacqueline Rycroft. When she began the business in 1976, in the premises next

door, little did Jacqueline know what a success she would have on her hands and, in 1996, she moved this present, purposed built, shop. There is everything the budding crafts person or artist could possibly want, including all manner of wools, embroidery threads, cottons and ribbons, artists materials, paper, modelling materials and various crafts kits. For those less ambitious, Jacqueline also stocks a wonderful selection of interesting and unusual gifts, from jewellery to cuddly toys. Village Crafts also offers an expert and fast framing service for their selection of original paintings and for customers own. What anyone coming here can be sure of too is a warm and friendly welcome from the staff and expert advice and knowledge regarding any handicraft problem they might have.

Village Crafts, The Square, Forest Row, East Sussex RH18 5ES Tel: 01342 823238

HAMMERWOOD
MAP 2 REF G3

7 miles NW of Crowborough off the A264

Here lies, down a potholed lane, **Hammerwood Park**, a splendid mansion that was built in 1792 by Benjamin Latrobe, the architect of the Capitol and the White House in Washington DC. Set within romantic parkland, the house has, over the years had a chequered time, including being the home of a member of the rock group Led Zeppelin in the 1970s and being rescued from ruin in the 1980s. Restoration work has been undertaken by the present owner and, whilst there are some massive murals in the hall, the dining room has been left derelict. The house is open on a limited basis during the summer.

HARTFIELD
MAP 2 REF G3

4 miles NW of Crowborough on the B2026

An old hunting settlement on the edge of the Ashdown Forest, which takes its name from the adult male red deer, or hart, the village is very closely associated with AA Milne and Winnie the Pooh. Milne lived at Cotchford Farm, just outside Hartfield and he set his famous books, which he wrote in the 1920s, in the forest. Designed to entertain his son, Christopher Robin, the books have been delighting children ever since and, with the help of illustrations by EH Shepard, the landscape around Hartfield has been brought to millions around the world.

In the village lies the 300 year old sweet shop to which Christopher Robin was taken each week by his nanny. Now called **Pooh Corner**, this is a special place to visit for both children and those who remember the stories from their own childhood. Full of Winnie the Pooh memorabilia, the shop caters for all tastes as long as it involves Winnie. All of the famous Enchanted Places lie within the parish of Hartfield and, **Poohsticks Bridge**, a timber bridge spanning a small tributary of the River Medway, was restored in 1979.

Found in the heart of this picturesque village is the attractive **Hay Waggon Inn**, a splendid country pub and restaurant that is housed in a building that is believed to date from 1540. Thought originally to have been a farmhouse, it has certainly been a hotel in the not too distant past, this magnificent building is now perfectly suited as a backdrop to this friendly village inn. Managed by licensees Simon Wilkinson and Michelle O'Rawe, this is where the old and the

The Hay Waggon Inn, High Street, Hartfield,
East Sussex TN7 4AB Tel: 01892 770252 Fax: 01892 770110

new meet. With open fires, agricultural memorabilia on the walls and hops hanging from the ceiling beams, the atmosphere throughout has a traditional air, but the high standard of hospitality is very much geared to the tastes of today's discerning customer. From the bar not only is there a fine selection of draught beers, ciders, bottled beers and wines, but customers can also enjoy a tasty bar snack throughout the day. Though more formal, the charming restaurant is the ideal place for a relaxing meal accompanied by fine wines. With several chefs in the kitchen putting together the delicious menu of homeprepared dishes for diners to savour it is not surprising that tables at The Hay Waggon are much sought after. Finally, this is not all this superb inn has to offer as they are also well known for their Monday monthly Jazz Evenings and other live music events.

Found on the edge of Ashdown Forest, **Honey Pots Olde English Tea Rooms and Stairs Farmhouse Bed and Breakfast** is a carefully modernised house that dates back to the 17TH century. Once owned by Adam Faith (in the 1970s), this splendid listed building is now the home of Susan and Brian Marion and their two daughters who provide a warm and friendly atmosphere for all their guests. The conservatory tea rooms, which overlook the large, well maintained gardens, is an excellent place to stop for some delicious homecooked refreshment.

**Honey Pots Olde English Tea Rooms and Stairs Farmhouse
Bed and Breakfast, Stairs Farmhouse, High Street, Hartfield,
East Sussex TN7 4AB Tel & Fax: 01892 770793**

As well as a wide assortment of teas, Honey Pots also has a license, and the magnificent aroma of baking cakes is sure to tempt anyone to apply themselves to the mouthwatering menu of sandwiches, light snacks, homemade soups and, of course, cakes. Those taking advantage of the bed and breakfast accommodation - there are three guest rooms - will find the same high level of hospitality is on offer. Each room is comfortably furnished and there are panoramic views through the windows out over Winnie the Pooh country.

WITHYHAM   MAP 2 REF G3
3½ miles NW of Crowborough on the B2110

This small village, with its church and pub, was also the home of the Sackville family from around 1200. The original village church was struck by lightning in 1663 that is said to have come in through the steeple, melted the bells and left through the chancel, tearing apart monuments on its route. Completely rebuilt, the landscape from the front of the church, over a stretch of grass and across fields to Hartfield in the distance is a view that has not changed for hundreds of years.

Inside the church is a large mural painted by an Earl De La Warr who was rector here in the 19ᵀᴴ century (the De La Warr family was a branch of the Sackville family) as well as a memorial to Vita Sackville-West, the poet and owner of Sissinghurst Castle in Kent who died in 1962.

BURWASH

Standing on a hill which is surrounded by land that is marsh for part of the year, Burwash is an exceptionally pretty village with a High Street that is chiefly lined with delightful 17ᵀᴴ and 18ᵀᴴ century timber framed and weatherboarded cottages. Among the buildings found here is **Rampyndene**, a handsome timber framed house with a sweeping roof that was built in 1699 for a wealthy local timber merchant. Burwash was, between the 15ᵀᴴ and 17ᵀᴴ centuries, a major centre of the Wealden iron industry and this brought much prosperity to the village.

However, it is not the village that brings most people to Burwash, though it certainly deserves the attention, but a house just outside. In 1902, Rudyard Kipling moved from Rottingdean to **Bateman's** to combat the growing problem of over enthusiastic sightseers. Located down a steep and narrow lane, the Jacobean house was originally built in 1634 for a prosperous local ironmaster and combined with its surrounding 33 acres of beautiful grounds -

Bateman's - Kiplings Home

landscaped by Kipling and his wife to complement the house - it proved the perfect retreat.

Kipling and his wife lived here until their deaths - he in 1936 and she just three years later - and during his time here the author wrote many of the famous works including *Puck of Pook's Corner*, the poem *If* and the Sussex poems. Now in the hands of the National Trust the rooms of the house have been left as they were when the Kiplings lived here and among the personal items on display is a watercolour of Rudyard Lake in Staffordshire, the place where his parents met and which they nostalgically remembered at the time of their son's birth out in Bombay. Also here are a series of terracotta plaques that were designed by Kipling's father, Lockwood Kipling, and used to illustrate his novel *Kim*. Lockwood was an architectural sculptor and went to India as the principal of an art school; he later became the curator of Lahore Museum.

Whilst here the Kipling's only son, John, was killed on active duty during World War I at Loos, France in 1915. There is a tablet to the 18 year old in the village church.

AROUND BURWASH

THREE LEG CROSS   Map 3 ref I4

4 miles N of Burwash off the B2099

In 1975, the Southern Water Authority dammed the River Bewl to create **Bewl Bridge Reservoir**, the largest area of inland water in the southeast of England. A great many buildings were lost under the water but one, the 15ᵀᴴ century **Dunsters Mill**, was taken down, brick by brick, before the waters rose and placed above the high water level. Another couple of timber framed farm buildings in the valley also found themselves uprooted and on their way to the Weald and Downland Museum at Singleton.

More than just a reservoir, the land around Bewl Bridge is a **Country Park** and has much

Bewl Bridge Resevoir

to offer including lakeside walks, trout fishing, pleasure boat trips and glorious countryside.

Built between 1385 and 1425 and reputed to be one of the oldest dwelling places in the country, **The Bull Inn** only became a pub towards the end of the 19ᵀᴴ century. A magnificent, ancient building, in a secluded location, the inn has a wealth of old beams, low ceilings and quarry tiled floors that give it a real

The Bull Inn, Three Leg Cross, Ticehurst, East Sussex TN5 7HH
Tel: 01580 200586 Fax: 01580 201289 website: www.thebullinn.co.uk

air of a traditional English country pub. A mass of small, intimate areas within, this is the place to come to for an excellent range of real ales, including their own brand - Bull's Best - and all the usual beers, ales and lagers. Food too is an important part of life here and the delicious homecooked dishes range from interesting, freshly prepared baguettes, to a full à la carte menu. Whether eating in warm and inviting dining room or outside in the large and attractive tree lined garden, a meal here is a treat well worth trying. Finally, the inn's friendly and hospitable hosts, Louise and Michael White, also offer relaxed and comfortable accommodation in a choice of four en suite guest rooms. A charming and delightful spot that is certainly worth finding.

TICEHURST

3½ N of Burwash on the B2099

MAP 3 REF I4

This ancient village is filled with attractive tile hung and white weatherboarded buildings that are so characteristic of the settlements along the Sussex and Kent border. Among the particularly noteworthy buildings here are **Furze House**, a former workhouse, and **Whatman's**, an old carpenter's cottage with strangely curving walls. The village is also home to **Pashley Manor Gardens**, which surround the Grade I listed timber frame house which dates from 1550. With waterfalls, ponds and a moat, these romantic gardens are typically English with numerous varieties of shrub roses, hydrangea and peonies adding colour and lushness at every corner. Less formally there is a woodland area and a chain of ponds that are surrounded by rhododendrons, azaleas and climbing roses. The gardens and house are privately owned but the gardens are opened on a limited basis.

ETCHINGHAM
MAP 3 REF I4

2 miles NE of Burwash on the A265

This scattered settlement, found in the broad lush valley of the River Rother, was home, in the Middle Ages, to the fortified manor of the de Echyngham family. Built to protect a crossing point on the River Rother, the house has long since gone though it stood where the village commuter station is now standing. Just outside the village lies **Haremere Hall**, an impressive 17TH century manor house that is now a centre for Shire horses. Several breeds of heavy horse are bred and trained here, including Shires, Clydesdales, Suffolk Punches and Ardennes and the combination of their sheer power and docility needs to be experience at first hand to be fully appreciated.

BRIGHTLING
MAP 3 REF I4

2½ miles S of Burwash off the B2096

The character of this tiny hillside village is completely overshadowed by the character of one of its former residents. It is certainly not unkind to say that the Georgian eccentric, 'Mad' Jack Fuller, was larger than life since he weighed some 22 stones and was affectionately referred to as the 'Hippopotamus'. A local ironmaster, squire and generous philanthropist, 'Mad' Jack was also sat as an MP for East Sussex between 1801 and 1812 and was elected only after a campaign that had cost him and his supporters a massive £50,000. Fuller was one of the first people to recognise the talents of a young painter, JMW Turner, and he was also responsible for saving Bodiam Castle from ruin.

However, it is for his series of imaginative follies that the colourful character is best remembered. He commissioned many of the buildings to provide work for his foundry employees during the decline of the iron industry and among those that remain today are Brightling Observatory, now a private house, a Rotunda Temple on his estate and the **Brightling Needle**. The 40 foot stone obelisk was built on a rise to the north of the village which is itself, 650 feet above sea level.

One of Fuller's more eccentric buildings was the result of a wager. Having bet with a friend on the number of spires that were visible from this home, Brightling Park, Fuller arrived back to find that, in fact, the steeple of Dallington church was not visible. In order to win the bet, Fuller quickly ordered his men to erect a 35 foot mock spire in a meadow on a direct line with Dallington and the monument is affectionately referred to as the **Sugar Loaf**. Perhaps, though Fuller's greatest structure is, in fact, his **mausoleum** which he built in the parish churchyard some 24 years before his death. A 25 foot pyramid, the story went around that Fuller was buried inside in a sitting position, wearing a top hat and holding a bottle of claret. However, despite the appropriateness of this image of his life, the parish church quashed the idea by stating that he was buried in the normal, horizontal pose.

NETHERFIELD

MAP 3 REF I5

5 miles S of Burwash on the B2096

Situated at Netherfield, to the south of Brightling, and with glorious views over the North Downs from the back and the South Downs from the front, **The Netherfield Arms** is an attractive 17th century country inn in a magnificent position. Well renowned for the splendid and colourful display of window boxes and flower filled troughs in the summer, this old building is also a sight in itself. Managed by Mike and Caroline Simpson, a local couple who have plenty of experience in the trade, The Netherfield Arms welcomes both locals and visitors alike. Inside, the building has a very traditional atmosphere, there are a mass of exposed beams, hop bines are displayed above the wooden bar, and there is a large inglenook fireplace decorated with gleaming horse brasses. As well as serving an excellent range of real ales, which changes regularly, and the

The Netherfield Arms, Netherfield Road, Netherfield, Battle, East Sussex TN33 9QD Tel: 01424 838282

usual beers and lagers, the inn also has a comprehensive wine list which covers both new and old world wines. However, it is as a restaurant that The Netherfield Arms is chiefly known. There are several delicious menus from which to choose, including a separate vegetarian and an à la carte. Local fish dishes, naturally, are a speciality but, with two chefs on hand, there are always plenty of mouth-watering homemade dishes to tempt the customer.

HERSTMONCEUX
MAP 3 REF H5

8 miles S of Burwash on the A271

The village is famous as being the home of **Herstmonceux Castle** which was built on the site of an early Norman manor house in 1440 by Sir Roger Fiennes. A remarkable building on two counts: it was one of the first large scale buildings in the country to be built of brick and it was also one of the first castles to combine the need for security with the comforts of the residents. As the castle was built on a lake there was added protection and the impressive gatehouse, with its murder holes and arrow slits, presented an aggressive front to any would be attackers.

Later, the castle passed into the hands of the Hare family, who presided over a long period of decline for

Herstmonceux Castle

Herstmonceux which culminated in most of the interior being stripped to provide building materials for another house in 1777. The castle sadly lay semi derelict for 150 years before a major programme of restoration was undertaken in the 1930s under the supervision of a Lewes architect, WH Godfrey. His careful and inspired work saw the turrets and battlements restored to their former glory and, today, the castle is as pristine as it was when first built in its delicious romantic setting.

In 1948, the Royal Observatory at Greenwich was looking for somewhere to move to away from the glow of the street lights of London. The Royal Observatory moved here and, after 20 careful years of planning and building, they opened the gigantic Isaac Newton telescope in the grounds. One of the five largest in the world it was officially opened in 1967. In 1989, the Royal Observatory moved again leaving the castle to become a conference centre. However, the castle is also home to the **Herstmonceux Science Centre**, where, among the domes and telescopes that the astronomers used between the 1950s and the 1980s, visitors can experience the excitement of viewing the heavens. There are also hands on displays and an Astronomy Exhibition which traces the history and work of the world famous Observatory.

Though the castle is not open to the public, **Herstmonceux Castle Garden**, the 500 acres of grounds around the splendid moated castle are open for most the year. Along with parkland and woodland there is an interesting Elizabethan garden.

HORAM

Map 3 ref H5

8 miles SW of Burwash on the A267

Situated beside the main road is a large cider press which at first seems strange in Sussex but was placed there by the makers of Merrydown cider when they came to the village in the 1940s.

Separate from, but on the estate of, Horam Manor is **Horam Manor Touring Park**, a tranquil rural caravan and camping site set in an area of outstanding natural beauty. Covering two gently sloping meadows, the pitches are of a generous size and the majority of them have electric hookups. Through each runs a tarmac and gravel access road. Ideal for children, as not only is this a safe place to play but the attractions of Horam Manor are close by. There is a special shower room for mothers and toddlers as well as other amenities including a laundry and a modern sanitary block. The family dog is welcome also and, with a nature trail running straight from the site, there is plenty to explore without leaving Horam Manor. Above all, the owners of this site, Mike, Joan, son Jonathan and Lynn, pride themselves on the high standards of cleanliness, the well maintained pitches and the relaxed and peaceful atmosphere that they provide for their visitors.

Horam Manor Touring Park, Horam, near Heathfield, East Sussex TN21 0YD Tel: 01435 813662 e-mail: horam.manor@virgin.net

WARBLETON
MAP 3 REF H5

6 miles SW of Burwash off the B2203

Found amongst a series of crisscrossing lanes, the village is little more than its church and a handful of houses. Inside the church is a magnificent galleried pew dating from the 18TH century that has two compartments on a level with the first floor. Whether these were used for checking the church attendance or for dozing off in during a dreary sermon no one is quite sure.

VINES CROSS
MAP 3 REF H5

7 miles SW of Burwash off the B2203

Lying in Vines Cross, just to the west of Warbleton, and with the motto 'A nice pub serving nice people', **The Brewers Arms** is sure to win the heart of anyone finding themselves enjoying the warm and friendly hospitality found here. First granted a license in 1753, this former blacksmith's cottage has always been known

**The Brewers Arms, Vines Cross, near Heathfield,
East Sussex TN21 9EN Tel: 01435 812288**

locally as The Clappers as the bridge over the nearby stream had loose boards and the hooves of horses crossing the bridge would make a clapping sound. Prior to today's hosts, Sussex born Carl and Kim Goldsmith taking over here, the pub was run by Carl's parents for 36 years and Maureen (Carl's mother) still helps out when needed. Carl's father, sadly, died a few years ago but his portrait can be seen of the pub sign outside.

As well as the large rear garden where there is a play area for children and also seating for adults, the interior of the pub is divided into various areas though each is as full of character and atmosphere as the others. The main bar, with its wood burning stove, has both flags and bicycles hanging from the ceiling and a library of books which customers are encouraged to exchange. The two other bar areas are much smaller and less eccentrically decorated though all are cosy and the ideal place to relax over a pint of real ale. Finally, The Brewers Arms is well known locally for the excellent menu of homecooked dishes that are on offer at both evening and lunchtime. Served in the Clappers Room, an intimate non smoking dining room with a marvellous collection of ceramic plates hanging from the walls, this is a treat that many customers travel some distance to savour.

CROSS IN HAND
MAP 3 REF H4
8 miles W of Burwash on the A267

This intriguingly named settlement lies on a busy road junction that has a post mill standing in the triangle formed by the converging roads. Certainly worth a second glance, the windmill at one time stood five miles away at Uckfield.

The **Cross-in-Hand Inn** is a part timbered public house and restaurant in the village that gives the pub its name. Dating back in parts to the 15TH century - as the exposed oak beams and wood panelling attest - this welcoming establishment has been renovated with great care and attention by Mo and Jackie Chatfield, the friendly and conscientious proprietors. The fine selection of real ales can be enjoyed in front of the crackling log fire in winter, or in the peaceful beer garden in summer. A big daily breakfast is served which includes all the favourites such as sausages, eggs, bacon, black pudding, mushrooms, toast all washed down with either tea or coffee. There is also a good choice of tasty

The Cross-in-Hand Inn, Cross in Hand, near Heathfield,
East Sussex TN21 0SN Tel: 01435 862053

lunches, bar snacks and evening meals available, seven days a week, and the sumptuous traditional Sunday lunch is a local legend. With pensioners perks and a smaller portions, small prices policy, the reasonably priced menus are sure to suit everyone. Ensure a table by booking in advance. For traditional home comforts and real value for money, The Cross-in-Hand is hard to beat.

CADE STREET
MAP 3 REF H4

5 miles W of Burwash on the B2096

This hamlet, that was used as a street market until the early 20ᵀᴴ century, is reputed to be the place where the notorious Jack Cade, leader of the Kentish rebellion, was killed in 1450 by the High Sheriff of Kent, Alexander Iden. A stone memorial marks the spot where he fell and on it is inscribed the moral: 'This is the Success of all Rebels, and this Fortune chanceth ever to Traitors.'

Situated in the glorious High Wealdean hamlet of Cade Street is **Spicers Bed and Breakfast**, a delightful place that is a Grade II listed cottage in part of a conservation area. The home of Valerie and Graham Gumbrell since 1980, this charming couple have been offering the very best in overnight accommodation

Spicers Bed and Breakfast, 21 Spicers Cottages, Cade Street, near Heathfield, East Sussex TN21 9BS Tel & Fax: 01435 866363 Mobile: 07973 188138 e-mail: spicersbb@compuserve.co.uk

since the summer of 1998. Though this was a cottage, it was a spacious one and many of the original features remain including the exposed beams and large inglenook fireplace in the guests' lounge. The letting rooms to have their own character and comprise a ground floor twin room with private shower room that is accessible to disabled guests and, on the first floor, a single en suite room and a wonderful double room with private bathroom. Each morning a delicious breakfast is served in the lounge complete with local sausages and local free range eggs though any dietary requirements can happily be catered for. With several pubs and restaurants within a small area, this is an ideal place to make for as a holiday base and, with glorious countryside right on the doorstep, guests will also enjoy relaxing in these pleasant surroundings.

HEATHFIELD
MAP 3 REF H5
6 miles W of Burwash on the A265

To the east of the town centre lies the large expanse of **Heathfield Park**, once owned by General Sir George Augustus Elliot (later Lord Heathfield), the Governor of Gibraltar and commander of the British garrison that successfully withstood attacks from both France and Spain between 1779 and 1782. Despite the wall surrounding the grounds, **Gibraltar Tower**, a castellated folly erected on his estate in his honour, can be seen.

Heathfield remained a quiet and undistinguished town until the arrival of the Tunbridge Wells to Eastbourne railway in the 19TH century and then it grew to become an important market town for the local area.

MAYFIELD
MAP 3 REF H4
6 miles NW of Burwash off the A267

This ancient settlement possesses one of the finest main streets in East Sussex and it is certainly one of the most picturesque villages in the area. According to local legend, St Dunstan, a skilled blacksmith by trade, stopped here in the 10TH century to preach Christianity to the pagan people of this remote Wealden community. Whilst working at his anvil, St Dunstan was confronted by the Devil who, disguised as a beautiful maiden, attempted to seduce the missionary. However, St Dunstan spotted that the feet of his young temptress were, in fact, cloven and, recognising her as Satan, grabbed her by the nose with a pair of red hot tongs. The Devil gave out an almighty scream and beat a hasty retreat; but he was soon to return, this time dressed as a traveller in need of new shoes for his horse. Dunstan again saw through the deception and, threatening Satan with his blacksmith's tools, forced him to promise never again to enter a house which had a horseshoe above the door.

St Dunstan went on to become the Archbishop of Canterbury in 959 and, some time later, **Mayfield Palace**, one of the great residences of the medieval Archbishops of Canterbury was built here. Though little remains of the grand palace now, a Roman Catholic Convent School incorporates the surviving buildings. Also, whilst he was living here, St Dunstan founded a simple timber church that was replaced by a stone structure in the 13TH century. After a fire and being struck by lightning, the present day **church of St Dunstan** is now a conglomeration of styles. Inside can be found a Jacobean pulpit, a font dated 1666 and some impressive 17TH and 18TH century monuments to the Baker family

WADHURST

MAP 3 REF H4

5 miles NW of Burwash on the B2099

This was another great centre of the Wealden iron industry in the 17TH and 18TH centuries and it was also one of the last places in Sussex to hold out against the improved coal fired smelting techniques which had taken root in the north. Though the village **church of St Peter and St Paul** is not quite built of iron the floor is almost entirely made up of iron tomb slabs, a unique collection which marks the graves of local ironmasters who died between 1617 and 1772.

The village was dominated by iron and many of Wadhurst's fine buildings date from the industries heyday, including the large Queen Anne vicarage, on the High Street, that was built by John Legas, the town's chief ironmaster. In the late 19TH century, the village sought fame when an important prize fights was held here with many of the spectators travelling from London to this rather obscure venue by train.

Built in the 1930s by a local brewery, **The Rock Robin** is a large brick and peg tiled inn that has ample space to accommodate the large local following it has gained over the years. However, despite its size, this is a cosy and intimate place with a real family feel. In fact, it is also a family run pub that is owned by Les and Mandy Bradley who are very ably helped by their son Mark and his girl friend Rachel. As well as the patio garden at the front of the building there is plenty of comfortable seating in the centrally located wood panelled bar area. Here, the atmosphere is very traditional as there is not only a Victorian wood burning stove (lit in the winter) but also, hanging from the ceiling, there are an

The Rock Robin, Station Hill, Wadhurst, East Sussex TN5 6RZ
Tel: 01892 783776

array of old carpenters' tools. The perfect place for those who enjoy a pint of real ale - there are always seven on tap - The Rock Robin is fast gaining an enviable reputation for the high standard of the meals that are served here in the separate restaurant. Everything is homecooked and the menu covers not only the traditional favourites but also a mouthwatering range of dishes from around the world, including Jamaican curry, Louisiana chicken, and a fantastic savoury filled crepe. This though is not all on offer at The Rock Robin as superb bed and breakfast accommodation is available in nine splendid en suite guest bedrooms.

TOURIST INFORMATION CENTRES

Locations in **bold** type are open throughout the year

Arundel
61 High Street, Arundel, West Sussex BN18 9AJ
Tel: 01903 882268 Fax: 01903 882419

Battle
88 High Street, Battle, East Sussex TN33 0AQ
Tel: 01424 773721 Fax: 01424 773436

Bexhill-on-Sea
51 Marina, Bexhill-on-Sea, East Sussex TN40 1BQ
Tel: 01424 732208 Fax: 01424 212500

Bognor Regis
Belmont Street, Bognor Regis, West Sussex PO21 1BJ
Tel: 01243 823140 Fax: 01243 820435

Boship
Boship Roundabout A22, Lower Dicker, Hailsham
East Sussex BN27 4DT Tel: 01323 442667 Fax: 01323 442667

Brighton
10 Bartholomew Square, Brighton, East Sussex BN1 1JS
Tel: 01273 292599

Burgess Hill
96 Church Walk, Burgess Hill, West Sussex RH15 9AS
Tel: 01444 247726 Fax: 01444 233707

Chichester
29a South Street, Chichester, West Sussex PO19 1AH
Tel: 01243 775888 Fax: 01243 539449

Crowborough

Tourism and Arts Section, Wealden District Council
Council Offices, Pine Grove, Crowborough, East Sussex TN6 1DH
Tel: 01892 602000 Fax: 01892 602566

Eastbourne

Cornfield Road, Eastbourne, East Sussex BN21 4QL
Tel: 01323 411400 Fax: 01323 649574

Gatwick

Airport International Arrivals, East Grinstead
West Sussex RH6 0NP Tel: 01293 579102

Hastings

Queens Square, Priory Meadow, Hastings, East Sussex
Tel: 01424 781111 Fax: 01424 781186

Horsham

9, The Causeway, Horsham West Sussex RH12 1HE
Tel: 01403 211661

Hove

Town Hall, Church Road, Hove, East Sussex BN3 3BQ
Tel: 01273 292539 Fax: 01273 293027

Lewes

187 High Street, Lewes, East Sussex BN7 2DE
Tel: 01273 483448 Fax: 01273 484003

Littlehampton

Windmill Complex, Littlehampton, West Sussex BN17 5LH
Tel: 01903 713480 Fax: 01903 713480

Midhurst

North Street, Midhurst, West Sussex GU29 9DW
Tel: 01730 817322 Fax: 01730 817120

Petworth

Market Square, Petworth, West Sussex GU28 0AF
Tel: 01798 343523 Fax: 01798 342743

Rye

The Heritage Centre, Strand Quay, Rye, East Sussex TN31 7AY
Tel: 01797 226696 Fax: 01797 223460

Seaford

25 Clinton Place, Seaford, East Sussex BN25 1NP
Tel: 01323 897426

Shoreham

Commerce Way, Lancing Business Park, Lancing, Shoreham-by-Sea
West Sussex Tel: 01273 263160 Fax: 01273 263131

Worthing

Chapel Road, Worthing, West Sussex BN11 1HL
Tel: 01903 210022 Fax: 01903 236277

INDEX OF TOWNS, VILLAGES AND PLACES OF INTEREST

Y

INDEX OF PLACES TO STAY, EAT, DRINK & SHOP

THE HIDDEN PLACES
ORDER FORM

To order any of our publications just fill in the payment details below and complete the order form *overleaf*. For orders of less than 4 copies please add £1 per book for postage and packing. Orders over 4 copies are P & P free.

Please Complete Either:

I enclose a cheque for £ .... made payable to Travel Publishing Ltd

Or:

Card No: ☐☐☐☐ ☐☐☐☐ ☐☐☐☐ ☐☐☐☐

Expiry Date: ☐☐☐

Signature: ....

NAME: ....

ADDRESS: ....

....

....

POSTCODE: ....

TEL NO: ....

Please send to:
Travel Publishing Ltd
7a Apollo House
Calleva Park
Aldermaston
Berks, RG7 8TN

THE HIDDEN PLACES
ORDER FORM

	Price	Quantity	Value
Regional Titles			
Cambridgeshire & Lincolnshire	£7.99	....	....
Channel Islands	£6.99	....	....
Cheshire	£7.99	....	....
Chilterns	£7.99	....	....
Cornwall	£7.99	....	....
Derbyshire	£7.99	....	....
Devon	£7.99	....	....
Dorset, Hants & Isle of Wight	£7.99	....	....
Essex	£7.99	....	....
Gloucestershire & Wiltshire	£7.99	....	....
Heart of England	£7.99	....	....
Hereford, Worcs & Shropshire	£7.99	....	....
Highlands & Islands	£7.99	....	....
Kent	£7.99	....	....
Lake District & Cumbria	£7.99	....	....
Lancashire	£7.99	....	....
Norfolk	£7.99	....	....
Northeast Yorkshire	£6.99	....	....
Northumberland & Durham	£6.99	....	....
North Wales	£7.99	....	....
Nottinghamshire	£6.99	....	....
Potteries	£6.99	....	....
Somerset	£7.99	....	....
South Wales	£7.99	....	....
Suffolk	£7.99	....	....
Surrey	£6.99	....	....
Sussex	£7.99	....	....
Thames Valley	£7.99	....	....
Warwickshire & West Midlands	£6.99	....	....
Yorkshire	£7.99	....	....
Set of any 5 Regional titles	**£25.00**	....	....
National Titles			
England	£9.99	....	....
Ireland	£9.99	....	....
Scotland	£9.99	....	....
Wales	£8.99	....	....
Set of all 4 National titles	**£28.00**	....	....
		_____	_____
		_____	_____

*For orders of less than 4 copies please add £1 per book for postage &
packing. Orders over 4 copies P & P free.*

THE HIDDEN PLACES
READER COMMENT FORM

The *Hidden Places* research team would like to receive reader's comments on any visitor attractions or places reviewed in the book and also recommendations for suitable entries to be included in the next edition. This will help ensure that the *Hidden Places* series continues to provide its readers with useful information on the more interesting, unusual or unique features of each attraction or place ensuring that their stay in the local area is an enjoyable and stimulating experience.

To provide your comments or recommendations would you please complete the forms below and overleaf as indicated and send to: The Research Department, Travel Publishing Ltd., 7a Apollo House, Calleva Park, Aldermaston, Reading, RG7 8TN.

Your Name:

Your Address:

Your Telephone Number:

Please tick as appropriate: Comments ☐   Recommendation ☐

Name of *"Hidden Place"*:

Address:

Telephone Number:

Name of Contact:

THE HIDDEN PLACES
READER COMMENT FORM

Comment or Reason for Recommendation:

....

....

....

....

....

....

....

....

....

....

....

....

....

THE HIDDEN PLACES
READER COMMENT FORM

The *Hidden Places* research team would like to receive reader's comments on any visitor attractions or places reviewed in the book and also recommendations for suitable entries to be included in the next edition. This will help ensure that the *Hidden Places* series continues to provide its readers with useful information on the more interesting, unusual or unique features of each attraction or place ensuring that their stay in the local area is an enjoyable and stimulating experience.

To provide your comments or recommendations would you please complete the forms below and overleaf as indicated and send to: The Research Department, Travel Publishing Ltd., 7a Apollo House, Calleva Park, Aldermaston, Reading, RG7 8TN.

Your Name:

Your Address:

Your Telephone Number:

Please tick as appropriate: Comments ☐   Recommendation ☐

Name of *"Hidden Place"*:

Address:

Telephone Number:

Name of Contact:

THE HIDDEN PLACES
READER COMMENT FORM

Comment or Reason for Recommendation:

....

....

....

....

....

....

....

....

....

....

....

....

MAP SECTION

The following pages of maps encompass the main cities, towns and geographical features of Sussex, as well as many of the interesting places featured in the guide. Distances are indicated by the use of scale bars located below each of the maps

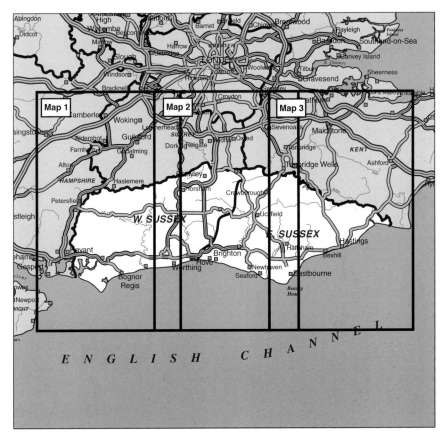

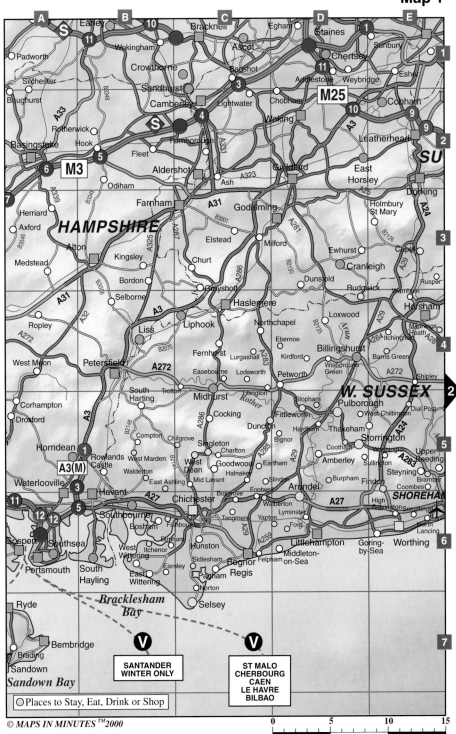

Map 1

© MAPS IN MINUTES ™ 2000

Map 2

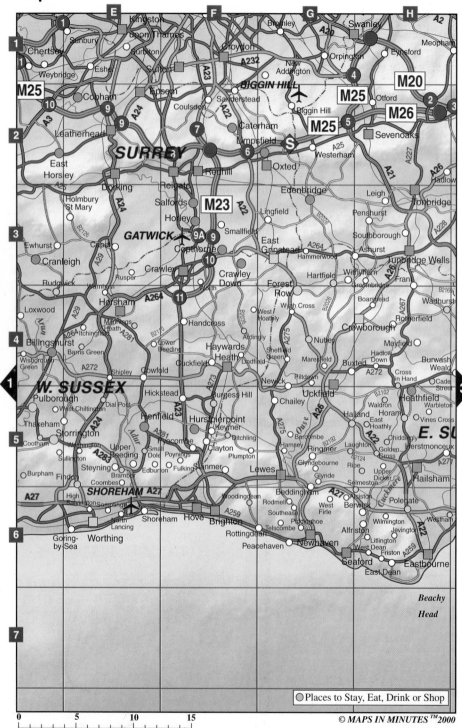

© MAPS IN MINUTES ™ 2000

Places to Stay, Eat, Drink or Shop

Map 3

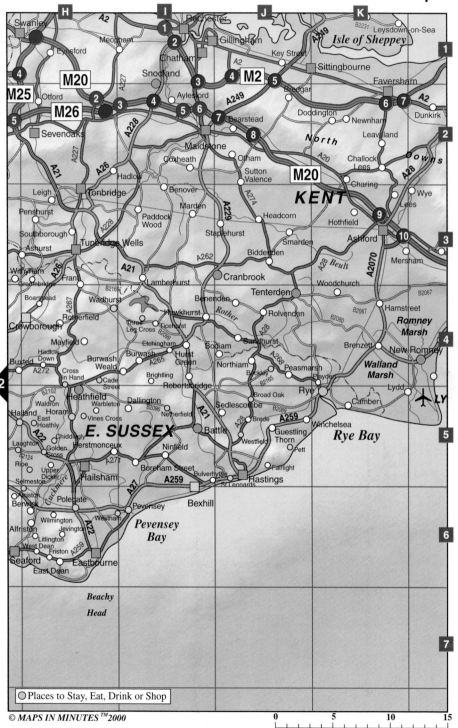